Inside THE DEEP tells the stories that will never be shown on camera—unique, and sometimes hair-raising episodes including

- Nick Nolte's death-defying "fall through" into the *Grifon* chamber, releasing in sequence thousands of pounds of rock, sand, debris—and Nick Nolte.

- The search for an authentic shipwreck to simulate the sunken *Goliath*.

- The construction of the world's largest and most complicated underwater set—a set which re-created the ocean floor and the interior of two sunken wrecks.

- The frenzied, feeding sharks and, especially, the "dead" seven-foot tiger shark who disrupted production when he unexpectedly came to life again.

- The casting call for a moray eel able to snap off a man's head on cue . . .

Inside THE DEEP

Inside
THE DEEP

by
Peter Guber
with
Barbara Witus

BANTAM BOOKS · LONDON · TORONTO · NEW YORK

INSIDE THE DEEP
A Bantam Book / July 1977

Front cover photograph copyright © 1976 by Howard Hall

*Back cover photograph copyright © 1977 by
Columbia Pictures Industries*

ISBN 0-553-11136-1

Published simultaneously in the United States and Canada

*Bantam Books are published by Bantam Books, Inc. Its trade-
mark, consisting of the words "Bantam Books" and the portrayal of a bantam, is registered in the United States Patent
Office and in other countries. Marca Registrada. Bantam
Books, Inc., 666 Fifth Avenue, New York, New York 10019.*

*To my wife Lynda, our family and all my friends
who gave me such support.*

Acknowledgment

This book would not have been possible without the unselfish efforts of Ms. Barbara Witus, Ms. Missy Alpern, Ms. Elisabeth Cox, Ms. Tommye Meyer and Marvin Levy whose invaluable assistance is deeply appreciated.

WHY ME?

I just produced my first feature film, a fact which still amazes me. And I live to tell about it, a fact which amazes me even more—because producing *The Deep* was the most exhausting, exhilarating, incredible adventure I've ever experienced.

Unlike most other avenues of life, where one day often seems to mesh insignificantly into the next, filmmaking is an intensified experience unto itself. During each production, all your energies, feelings, and time are focused on one specific goal: making the movie. Of course, making the movie *good* is something else entirely, and it's not always easy to measure how you're doing. No movie is an automatic win/lose proposition, but when you're wrapped up in making it, it sure seems like one. You're always aware that later a minute error in judgment will show up in Panavision dimensions of sixty feet high and a hundred and forty feet wide on film screens all over the world, to haunt you for the rest of your life. On the other hand, the final product could be a huge success, the achievement of a lifetime. These great risks and simultaneously great possibilities are what make filmmaking such an intensive undertaking.

All this behind-the-scenes agonizing doesn't make much difference to the final judges, the audiences. As long as it's *believable,* most moviegoers don't care how rigorous the experience or revolutionary the technology was that went into a film. Consequently, if *The Deep* could have been filmed with just an Instamatic camera in a bathtub with scuba-suited kewpie dolls—and filmed *right*—believe me, I would have been right there with my rubber duck! But it couldn't. The filming of *The Deep* called for a massive collaborative effort involving the talents and skills of hundreds of people from all over the world; many millions of dollars; and eighteen grueling months of work, including many six- and seven-day weeks. Nearly one hundred full days were spent underwater in four oceans all over the world by four actors and their director who had never dived before; there were thousands of individual dives and man-hours spent underwater; over a million cubic feet of compressed air were breathed by our team during its filming . . . the arithmetic alone of *The Deep* is pretty mind-boggling. The sum total of all these ingredients—audience reaction—is the only uncertainty at this time, and you can believe we're all holding our breaths!

But whatever it is, making *The Deep* was a once-in-a-lifetime challenge for all concerned. And "writing" this book during its production was a unique private challenge for me. My habit of stealing away to "talk to myself"—of keeping a taped diary of sorts during production—led many of my colleagues to conclude that the pressures of filming were *really* getting to me! But it was a good release of tension for me at the time and served later as the basis for the book you are about to read. I hope you find it informative and entertaining, for I think it succeeds to a large extent in capturing the essence of feature filmmaking as I experienced it during this production and, hopefully, in shedding some light on that curious and unparalleled adventure called filmmaking: a study in paranoia and hope.

If you do, then I accomplished to some degree what I set out to do, and my double tour of duty was worth it.

Peter Guber
Hollywood, California
January 1977

CAST AND CREW LIST

Cast:
Robert Shaw
Jacqueline Bisset
Nick Nolte
Louis Gossett
Eli Wallach
Robert Tessier
Earl Maynard
Bob Minor
Lee McClain
Teddy Tucker
Dick Anthony Williams

Screenplay by Peter Benchley and Tracy Keenan Wynn
Based on the novel by Peter Benchley
Produced by Peter Guber
Directed by Peter Yates

Crew:
Supervising Film Editor ....Robert L. Wolfe
Production Designed by ....Tony Masters
Director of Photography ....Christopher Challis, B.S.C.
Second Unit Underwater Directors ....
....Al Giddings/Stan Waterman
Second Unit Underwater Cinematographers ....
....Al Giddings/Stan Waterman
Underwater Lighting ....Christopher Challis
Underwater Production ....Al Giddings
Underwater Third Camera ....Chuck Nicklin
Underwater Grip ....Gordon Waterman
Project Electrical Technician ....Wulf Koehler
Dive Master ....Dennis Breese
Underwater Grip ....Jack Monestier
Underwater Camera Control ....Bob Cecchini
Dive Equipment Coordinator ....Van Worley
Underwater Continuity ....Geri Murphy
Underwater Camera Housings by ....Al Giddings

Captain Dive Boat—British Virgin Islands ....Moby Griffin
Captain Dive Boat—Australia ....Wally Mueller
Surgeon to Underwater Team ....Don Buehler, M.D.
Underwater Set Dresser ....Peter Grant
Marine Environments by ....Carlos Machado
Marine Biologists ....Kym Murphy/John Hart

Special Underwater Stereo Recording ....Robin Gregory
Underwater Still Photographer ....David Doubilet
Associate Producer ....George Justin
Special Consultant ....Teddy Tucker

Art Director ....Jack Maxsted
Set Decorator ....Vernon Dixon

Production Manager ....George Justin
First Assistant Director ....Derek Cracknell
Key Second Assistant Director ....Richard Jenkins
Second Assistant Director ....Raymond Becket
Production Executive ....Peter A. Lake

Special Effects ....Ira Anderson, Jr./Ira Anderson, Sr./
Charles Spurgeon/Gene Cornelius/Don Puck/
Steve DeSilva
Stunt Coordinators..Bob Minor/James Nickerson/Max Kleven
Camera Operator ....John Palmer
Construction Manager ....Dick Frift
Sound Recordist ....Robin Gregory
Continuity ....Mary Dalison/Sally Jones
Surface Still Photographer ....Keith Hamshere

Costume Designer ....Ron Talsky
Wardrobe ....Tom Bronson
Wardrobe Assistants ....Tina Hutchins/Tom Watlington
Hair Dresser ....Pat McDermott
Make Up ....Ed Henriques/Bob Dawn

Follow Focus ....Tony Strachan
Clapper/Loader ....David Budd
Key Grip ....Ron Lenior
Camera Grip ....Pat Newman
Assistant Construction Manager ....Bert Bowers
Carpenters ....Fred Morris/Geoff Kingsley
Key Electrician ....Ron Pearce
Best Boys ....Fred Bradley/Ron Webster

Property Master ....Graham Sumner
Electricians ....Peter Casey/Peter Martin/Derek Gatrell
Best Boy Grip ....Roy O'Connor
Supervising Plasterer ....George Gilliard
Fiberglass Plasterer ....Jack Arnott
Supervising Painter ....Fred Heyes
Scenic Painter ....Bill Beecham
Scenic Designer ....Eddie Lima
Property ....Terry Wells/Barry Wilkinson
Property/Set Dressing ....John Hogan/Les Benson
Assistant Art Director ....Alan Cassie
Film Editor ....David Berlatsky
Assistant Film Editors ....Mike Klein/Ron Fagin/
Carol Jackson/Penny Shaw
Boom Operator ....Terry Sharratt

Sound Maintenance Engineer ....Michael Harris
Assistant to the Set Decorator ....Lynda Guber
Supervising Project Manager ....Marvin J. Levy
Assistant to the Project Manager ....Elisabeth Cox
Production Coordinator ....Richard Liebegott
Production Accountant ....Vince Martinez
Assistant to the Accountant ....Rita Harthorn
Location Manager ....Peter Bieler
Assistant to the Producer ....Bill Rudin
Assistant to the Director ....Mike Nathanson
Assistant to the Production Manager ....Sam Gellis
Secretary to the Producer and Director ....Missy Alpern
Special Sound Consultant ....Hal Landaker

Additional
Post-Production Personnel ......Marilyn Madderom/Don Wolfe/
Flo Williamson

Music by ....John Barry

"The Deep" was filmed live on location in four oceans, and
we gratefully acknowledge the following contributions:
    The government and the people of the British Virgin
        Islands, Bermuda and Australia
    The Smithsonian Institute
    Peter Island Yacht Club
    Southampton Princess Hotel
    Van Cleef & Arpels for replication of 17th Century treasure

FLASHBACK

July 5, 1976

Portion of a transoceanic radio telephone conversation between Hollywood, California, and Peter Island, British Virgin Islands:

"How's it going out there, Peter?"

"Oh, great, David. Terrific."

"Have you gone down yet?"

"Well, no, not yet. I—"

"Don't you think you should, to see what's going on down there?"

"Right. You're absolutely right . . ."

"David" was David Begelman, President of Columbia Pictures. "Peter" was me, Peter Guber, film producer of Peter Benchley's novel, *The Deep*. And "down there" was the huge hundred-year-old shipwreck in the Caribbean on which we had begun our authentic underwater location filming. David was right: as producer of the film, I *should* visit our location, even if it was lying under eighty feet of Caribbean brine. There was only one minor problem: I was deathly afraid of water.

"Now, whatever you do, remain calm. This is a demand-type regulator, so you must suck in order to get your air. If you feel like you're out of air, don't panic."

I was receiving my diving initiation in the Peter Island Yacht Club pool, bobbing next to the local instructor, Murray Maxwell. I nodded vigorously as he spoke, even as I incredulously repeated his advice in my mind. "If you run out of air don't panic?" I thought. "Who's he kidding?"

It was time to test me in the real undersea world, Murray decided, and now it was almost impossible to hide my panic. On the ocean, the water looked dark blue and choppy, not at all inviting. Enclosed in the clammy rubber of the wet-suit, with unfamiliar equipment on my back, the harness and full air tank seemed to weigh a ton. Lead weights draped my waist. I gritted my teeth and jumped overboard after Murray. I felt like a newborn kitten being licked by a Great Dane. I sputtered and swallowed some salt water as I slipped below the ocean's surface . . . into the deep.

My breath rang hollowly in my ears. My jaws ached from gripping the mouthpiece. I began to descend. Five feet, ten feet, twenty feet down into the blue, silent world below. I repeated Murray's instructions to myself like a holy incantation. Equalize air pressure in ears; clear mask; breathe deeply; don't panic. Panic? I was beyond panic. In fact, I had one very lucid thought as I descended into the waters of the Caribbean.

"What in hell am I doing here?"

It wasn't the first time I'd asked that question, and it wasn't to be the last. Making Peter Benchley's second novel into a film was one frightening plunge after another; this adventure in the Caribbean had simply been the wettest so far. Not only had I never dived before, I'd never produced a motion picture. And learning to produce by making *The Deep* was kind of like learning to fly by taking up a 747.

Not that I was a total naif when the madness began. I'd been part of the film industry for years. My career started, in fact, when I was a college student plastered with degrees from various institutions of higher learning. Bright-eyed and bushy-tailed, I began as a trainee at Columbia Pictures straight from Business school. I worked like a demon. After about three months, I knew I wanted to leave and produce motion pictures myself. But I hung in for eight more years.

In that time, I worked my way up to the post of Executive Vice President in Charge of World-Wide Production. I was the liaison between the studio and the actual film productions it parented, overseeing project development, production, and post-production. It was a position of executive power and ego satisfaction, but I'd experienced all I could where I was. It was time to move on, to test myself on the other end—to be more directly involved in the creative process of making films. It was a frightening decision to make, but finally the time was right. It was just a little under two years ago as of this writing; it now feels more like a century.

A production deal was hammered out over a period of weeks that made me an independent film producer affiliated with Columbia. That meant that I would develop and produce films subject to Columbia's approval, for which, in turn, they would provide funds and facilities as necessary. "Peter Guber's Filmworks," my new company, was born. And then, boom—it was out of the executive offices and into a temporary set-up in the Columbia building until permanent facilities were readied.

Suddenly I felt like a baby bird who's been restless to try his wings, but becomes frozen with fear when he's tossed out of the nest. The hundreds of phone calls I'd been getting every day immediately dwindled to ten or twelve. I had been a big deal as an executive, but as a producer, I was back to square one. Worse, there were plenty of people in the industry who thought my new status as independent producer was Columbia's way of easing me out. Some film executives are put out to pasture via producers' settlements; the studio's commitment gradually diminishes, one day stopping altogether.

So I had to somehow quickly establish credibility for my new company. Not only because my ego smarted at the thought of all the barracudas in the industry thinking the worst, but because without credibility I couldn't produce movies, at least not the films I wanted to be involved with.

The way to accomplish this goal was to acquire a "big" project: a glossy, high-visibility property that would immediately establish my company as a force to contend with in the competitive film industry. It would give Filmworks the image of power, and in Hollywood, as in other businesses, that image often *is* power. Just as I was beginning my scouting expedition, the author of one of the smash hits of all time was finishing his second novel. Peter Benchley, scion of the Benchley family—his father is novelist Nathaniel Benchley, his grandfather was the humorist Robert Benchley—had knocked the worlds of publishing and film on their ears with his first novel, *Jaws*. I heard that Benchley was now putting the finishing touches on his second novel, and my ears perked up.

Needless to say, I wasn't the only one. Peter Benchley had made himself a sackful of money on *Jaws*—something in the vicinity of several million dollars, between hardcover and paperback sales and his percentage of the film's profits. But he'd also made several other people fabulously wealthy as well. So you can believe that his literary activities were being monitored attentively by all the interested folks who hoped, naturally, that lightning would strike twice. Benchley's fortunes were being directed by International Creative Management, which is one of the two biggest theatrical agencies in the business, thereby wielding a tremendous amount of clout in the film industry. Benchley was an important enough client of theirs to be pampered by not one, but three representatives: Marvin Josephson, President of ICM; Jeff Berg, aggressive fair-haired wunderkind of the company, both literally and figuratively; and Roberta Pryor, Peter's dynamic agent in ICM's New York office. The second novel, at this point not even definitely titled *The Deep* yet, had been quickly snatched up in the preliminary stages by Doubleday for publishing. They paid a lot more up front this time around than the $7,500 they'd paid Peter originally for *Jaws*. Now it was time to peddle the property to Hollywood. In the old days, a book would be published before film rights were sold. But now these transactions are made earlier and earlier, and the film and publishing industries have become very cozy with each other, to their mutual benefit. In fact, it's all come full circle, with "novelizations" of original Hollywood films being published as books!

Naturally, Peter Benchley and ICM had a tender spot in their hearts for Richard Zanuck and David Brown, the producers who, with director Steven Spielberg, had done such a handsome and lucrative job of translating *Jaws* to film. It's customary in the entertainment business to give the buyer of an author's property the first look at whatever he or she writes next. But ICM had a responsibility to their client to make the best deal possible. So Zanuck and Brown were offered first refusal, but supposedly with the stipulation that they would not negotiate the asking price of $1,000,000 for the film rights to the book, plus $250,000 for Benchley's screenwriting services, *plus* a large percentage of the film's profits.

Now, any industry that will pay $400,000 simply for the right to translate a literary property into a movie will not necessarily be known for its prudence. But, Zanuck and Brown, while running Twentieth Century-Fox, had paid that much for the purchase of *Butch Cassidy and the Sundance Kid,* and they made a killing. That was a few years ago already, and Hollywood, like every other industry, suffers from inflation. Still, a million dollars is a million dollars, and that's a lot of money anywhere, even in Hollywood. Zanuck and Brown declined. ICM was now free to sell the property to the highest bidder.

October 20, 1976

I'd been watching these goings-on very carefully, and when Z & B passed, I seized the initiative. My Columbia background proved invaluable. Without it, I'd hardly have stood a chance of seeing the galleys in time to participate. In spite of my professional friendship with Marvin Josephson, it took some creative cajoling, but Josephson and Berg finally sent the galleys. The accompanying note said they'd like to know my reaction as soon as possible, since "We anticipate quite a bit of interest." What that meant, of course, was, "We anticipate a stampede." So I raced home with the prize and eagerly began reading *The Deep,* at that time only a sheaf of 336 pages piled into a gray cardboard box. And when I finished reading at 3 A.M., I knew this was it.

The Deep is the story of a young couple honeymooning in Bermuda. They are swept up in a whirlpool of danger and intrigue when exploring the shipwreck of the *Goliath,* a merchant ship sunk in a hurricane in 1943. They stumble headlong onto a long-hidden cache of illegal drugs. Lying beneath the iron wreck of the *Goliath* is something else. David and Gail, our young newlyweds, discover a Spanish treasure piece so valuable as to defy logic. Theirs is the quest to uncover what is down in the Deep, why it's there and get it up. In doing this they are forced by circumstance into an unholy alliance with Romer Treece, a Bermudian treasure expert, recluse and living legend. *The Deep* is the story of what they go after . . . and what goes after them.

While the tale lacked, as one critic would later put it, "the maxillary crunch of *Jaws*," it was a good, compelling story in its own right, and the filmic possibilities practically leaped off the pages. *The Deep* was also that high-profile project that would immediately establish my company. And *The Deep* had another important point in its favor: it was very likely to get made. In Hollywood, a miss is as good as a mile, and what you don't make doesn't count. The amount of paper used in scripts and books that are bought and never actually turned into movies would, if converted back to trees, put the Black Forest to shame. But a high-visibility project by the man who wrote the blockbuster *Jaws*? Somehow, sowewhere, it would actually get filmed. And I wanted to be the one to produce it.

Now, to say a property is certain to be made doesn't necessarily mean it's going to be *easy* to make. And *The Deep* promised to be anything but. Hollywood can create almost anything on a 35mm strip of film, but certain things can't be directed by the simple commands, "Lights, camera, action!" One of these is animals, especially when they are supposed to be wild —and they are. Weather is another, and a particularly agonizing ingredient when millions of dollars are staked on it. But the worst, the very worst of all the taboos is water—Public Enemy Number One in filmmaking, to be avoided whenever possible. Filming *The Deep* would involve all three. The warning flags were at full mast.

If I'd actually had first-hand experience with any water-based production at the time, I probably wouldn't have touched *The Deep*. Many difficulties of making *The Deep* were obvious. But above all, although I had changed jobs, desks, and even some friends—my old nemesis, common fear, was still my constant companion. It was such a big film! I could triumph, but I could really take a bath in *The Deep,* too.

Well, it was either sink or swim, or in this case, dive. I decided to "go for it."

Timing was of the essence; we would have to move decisively if we were interested in acquiring the property. President of Columbia David Begelman read the manuscript and threw full support behind the purchase of *The Deep;* so, happily, did Production Vice Presidents John Veitch and Bill Tennant, who would turn out to be the front man in the deal-making. My former position at Columbia had not yet been filled, but the new V.P. turned out to be Stanley Jaffe, another *Deep* enthusiast from the beginning and throughout the grueling months that would follow.

Trying to get two enormous corporations to enter into a giant financial transaction on my behalf required more than expertise at filmmaking or entrepreneurial skill—a carnival barker's touch was also indispensable to maintain a fever pitch of excitement at Columbia about *The Deep.* Learning that Bantam Books had bought paperback rights for three quarters of a million dollars, I artfully spread the word. The issue of a novel in paperback and its potential success closely parallel the potential mass market success of a film. I circulated a list of competitive interest which was not only informative, but inflammatory. After all, whatever you want looks that much better if someone else wants it too. Certainly this is so in Hollywood. In spite of some negative opinions, Columbia decided to go after rights to *The Deep* seriously, with the express intent of keeping the acquisition price in hand. If other potential buyers found out that Columbia was vigorously pursuing the book, they might leap into the fray, creating an auction environment that could push the price sky-high. ICM was to be given a major offer if they agreed to negotiate with no one else until a satisfactory conclusion had been reached one way or another within a specified period of time.

By now Bill Tennant had engineered his game plan

for the purchase of the book. He reasoned that, with his huge take from *Jaws,* Peter Benchley was not exactly hurting for money. So our thrust should be an appeal to Benchley's ego rather than to his wallet, in the form of a "star deal"—that is, one in which the emphasis would be on the idea that we were buying *Peter Benchley*— his name, his talents—not merely a literary property of his. It was a good approach, but the powerful agents at ICM could be counted on to go after the maximum in dollars, at least partly because their 10 percent commission on the sale, if based on Benchley's ego alone, wouldn't keep *their* refrigerators stocked. And so the negotiations began.

It sometimes seems a hallmark of deal-making that the more money is at stake, the more disembodied the actual transaction. No yelling back and forth in smoke-filled boardrooms or nose-to-nose, slit-eyed confrontations in plush restaurants here. This deal took form from a series of phone calls whizzing back and forth over a distance of eight thousand miles. Marvin Josephson was in Hawaii; Jeff Berg, Bill Tennant, and I were in Los Angeles; David Begelman, Peter Benchley, and Roberta Pryor were in New York. The formal negotiations were actually completed within forty hours. Not directly involved in the dealings, I became a one-man rooting section, peanut gallery, and cattle prodder, watching anxiously from the sidelines, running in and out of Bill Tennant's office to see how it was going, calling for support from allies across the country.

November 5, 1976

Meanwhile, representatives of the two chief industry trade papers, *Variety* and *Hollywood Reporter,* were breathing down our necks, each vying to scoop the other on the deal. There is a Hollywood axiom which holds that if two people know something, one of them will leak it to the trades. We had to try to hold them at bay while completing the transaction: a premature leak could abort our still-embryonic deal. And since this was to be Filmworks' first acquisition, I wanted to see the story come out as a carefully worded publicity release geared for maximum impact, not some guy's morning scoop.

Well, no such luck. The deal was closed on November 5, 1975, at 10:30 A.M. Benchley would receive over a half-million dollars, depending upon his activity in the film, the success of the book, and other ingredients. He'd also receive a healthy percentage of the gross from the movie. By 11:15 the trade papers had all the pertinent information on their own, and Columbia, backed into a corner, could only confirm the acquisition.

News of the purchase had maximum impact anyway. The reactions in the industry were diverse—but everyone reacted. Some observers were genuinely congratulatory; some amazed; others jealous. Any number of those in the Hollywood rumor mill cattily concluded that the book would flop, and probably the film too. Filmworks and *The Deep* were rolling—and everyone, catty or not, was now watching curiously to see what I would do next.

To tell you the truth, so was I.

1
CHARTING A COURSE

I am now the proud owner of a slick, expensive movie property that could easily turn into one gigantic, glossy white elephant.

Peter Benchley is not a goose, of course. But the fact is that he has produced one gorgeous golden egg in *Jaws*. Whether his second effort, *The Deep,* will do as well—even half as well would be terrific—we won't know for months. In the meantime, I somehow have to get the production going in an atmosphere compounded equally of high expectations and high skepticism.

What everybody wants, of course, publishers and studio both, is a best seller, which will help lay the foundation for a hit movie, which in turn will help the best seller become even *more* of a best seller. You can bet that Doubleday, Bantam, and Columbia are determined to launch the total media event called *The Deep* as carefully as NASA launches a space missile, and in stages that are just as precisely timed. It's now December, 1975. The hardcover edition of the novel will be published by Doubleday in May, 1976. Bantam will allow time for maximum circulation of the hardback before coming out with their paperback edition, and the film should come along about three months later, thereby scooping up both hardcover and softcover readers. All this works out to a release date for *The Deep* of June, 1977.

June, 1977 sounds like a long way away from December, 1975—but we worked backward from that date and realized that we'll have to begin shooting on July 1, 1976. A fantastically complex and expensive motion picture will have to be completely readied for filming in just about six months!

Usually, when you're mounting a motion picture, you're working from a final or near-final shooting script. The script not only attracts key members of cast and crew, but serves as a guideline for determining the necessary production elements; such as locations, sets, and props. With a near-final draft it usually takes a minimum of six months to assemble all these elements. In the case of *The Deep,* though, preproduction time is already very tight and page one of the script has not even been written. All we have are the outlines of the story as set forth in the novel—and the fact that *The Deep* has been written by the author of *Jaws.*

Anyone who reads the book can see immediately that *The Deep* cannot even remotely be construed as a "sequel" to *Jaws*—and any attempt to market it as such could backfire royally. In fact, the two books, beyond the fact that they are both set on and in the ocean, are entirely different. The *Jaws* association, however, is a potent one in the film industry, and with an unpublished book and an unwritten script, it's our only real ace in the hole. After all, if Columbia Pictures has been sold on *The Deep* mostly on the basis of the success of its predecessor, then the property could attract the top industry talent it needs in the same way. It *has* to.

The first step is to find a director as quickly as possible, to give the project both momentum and the creative input necessary at this stage of the game. Columbia wants an experienced person at the helm of this film to help protect their investment. Our director will have to be a thorough professional who understands what it takes to get a film made—not just artistically, but in nuts-and-bolts production terms, too. He must have worked with major stars and shot at least one action-adventure film which demonstrates an understanding of the genre. Experience on big-budget films would be a plus. Last but not least, since so much of *The Deep* takes place on, in, and around water, it would help if he has worked with this uniquely exasperating element.

Only a handful of directors meet all those requirements, among them, Franklin Schaffner, Peter Yates, Steven Spielberg, John Frankenheimer, John Boorman. Most of them, just as I'd feared, are already deep in the throes of preproduction, production or post-production on various other films—a situation not surprising in an industry where top talent is often committed to projects a year or two in advance. It's also most likely a harbinger of the crunch we'll suffer later, when we're trying to put together an illustrious cast just two months before the start of filming.

Peter Yates is momentarily between films. Peter is the elegant Englishman who first hit in the United States with his direction of the action classic, *Bullitt,* starring Steve McQueen. Since then, Yates has done several other American films, including *The Hot Rock, The Friends of Eddie Coyle, John and Mary, For Pete's Sake* and *Mother, Jugs and Speed.* Yates also directed *Murphy's War,* a well-mounted multi-million dollar action movie set on and near the water, and an especially appropriate prelude to *The Deep.* Yates' career as a director is an interesting one that reveals a wide range of experience and an openness to collaboration. Action-adventure is Yates' forte, and as he himself agrees, he's ready for a "big" film. Not that he's been twiddling his thumbs waiting for us to come along—he already has two projects in development and a firm offer to direct *The Eagle Has Landed.* But Peter is intrigued with *The Deep,* and I've got my fingers crossed.

I just heard that he read the galleys last night and has refused his other offers. Yates will direct our project! Now *I* had a partner and I became *we.*

Peter Benchley just flew in for the first of several intensive script meetings. Poor Peter Benchley. As much as he loves to dive, he loathes flying, and each flight is a real trial for him. Seclusion at home in Princeton, New Jersey, and writing bestselling novels is more to his taste.

January 25, 1976

The Deep poses some thorny problems in the transition from book to film. The novel features a complicated interweaving of plots, all revolving around the sunken caches of drugs and treasure, that will have to be simplified and focused. The numerous background stories that set up these plots will have to find cinematic—that is, visual, rather than verbal—counterparts on the screen. And nearly 50 per cent of the story's action takes place underwater: a world that is visually disorienting, and one in which characters can barely communicate—a world that could puzzle and alienate our viewers as easily as it could fascinate them. The underwater action will have to be broken down, analyzed, and carefully reworked into the script to provide the maximum in both clarity and suspense.

February 3

All this would be a pretty tall order for any screenwriter. For Benchley, it has its own special challenge and grief. It's not easy for a novelist to hear his own work dissected in terms of whether or not it'll "play" on screen. And it's notoriously hard for an author to come to grips with his own material in the writing of a screenplay. Benchley is a delight to work with: receptive to ideas, open to collaboration, not at all defensive. Whether he can make the significant changes that are vital to the success of the screenplay still remains to be seen.

Benchley has flown back east to huddle over his loyal typewriter, and Yates and I are turning our attention to another nagging problem: Just where are we going to film *The Deep*? We have to lock into a location as soon as possible. Everything else—sets, budget, even final script —depends on it. The story is set in Bermuda, but that doesn't necessarily mean that Bermuda is the automatic location choice. It's not simply the physical setting you take into account when planning a location shoot, but a grabbag of other factors, too: transportation, communication, housing, convenience of film labs, and the cost—of everything. Expenses add up at the speed of light on location, and even small cost differences at the beginning can balloon quickly. With all these factors in mind, we've compiled brochures and clippings on every place we can think of that might serve us well as an ersatz Bermuda. We've investigated the possibilities of Florida, the Bahamas, Jamaica, and even Catalina, a small island right off the California coast.

Our final decision, however, is, happily, the most desirable. Besides authenticity, we're discovering that the tiny British island of Bermuda has other points in favor of our filming there, too.

The island is off by itself in the middle of nowhere —way out in the Atlantic Ocean, almost midway between Los Angeles and London. On the map, it looks like a cartographer's accidental inkblot, due east of North Carolina and about 750 miles southeast of New York. It sounds remote, but by jet Bermuda is reachable via New York or Boston in just about an hour and a half.

Not only does that mean that cast and crew can get there with relative ease, but that "dailies," the footage generated each day during filming, can quickly make the trip to the New York film labs. Phone connections between Bermuda and the United States are excellent —you can even dial direct between the two. The island's location places it in a time zone only one hour later than that of New York—another communications plus. As a popular resort, the island boasts a wealth of sophisticated hotels and inns. And the fact that Bermuda is a foreign country means that we can use an English crew, at a considerable savings over what an American crew would cost.

All in all, this little spot of a country just might be able to play itself in *The Deep*. Yates, Benchley, and I are in the air, heading for Bermuda this February night to find out, accompanied by two new *Deep* staffers.

George Justin has been commissioned as Production Manager and Associate Producer. In this business of making illusions, the Production Manager is in charge of reality, responsible for all the logistical and financial details that constantly threaten to derail a picture unless kept firmly on track. George, with more than thirty years of experience in every facet of the film industry, is perfect for the job.

February 12

A young writer-photographer-filmmaker named Peter Lake was hired to be our "Production Executive," a catchall title for a variety of crucial duties. Peter is acquainted with many facets of movie-making, especially the problems unique to underwater film production. His credits include the shark documentary, *Blue Water, White Death*—even so far as taking the spectacular still that became that movie's advertising campaign.

Well, we landed a couple of hours ago, and did Bermuda have a few surprises in store for us! The first was the weather, which we had assumed would be warm and sunny. Although it's far from the equator, around which most professional paradises are huddled, Bermuda is blessed with semitropical temperatures, courtesy of the warming Gulf Stream. Our assumption was based on this knowledge and the assurance of the Bermuda Department of Tourism that "Bermuda has only two seasons—summer and not-quite-summer."

Well, what we stepped into from the plane was considerably closer to not-quite-winter. Cold. Drizzly. Gray. We gritted our teeth and tried to ignore it. After all, we'll be filming in summer, not winter, when the weather will be balmy and beautiful. We anticipate only two major problems with that ideal summer weather—hurricanes, a harrowing consideration all through preproduction and actual filming, and tourists, with which Bermuda will be bursting.

Even through the February gray that framed our first look at it, we could see Bermuda's beauty and charm. But we have to find as many specific physical locations as we can that will fit the requirements of the story. Bermuda offers several; in fact, many of the settings Benchley wrote into the novel are modeled after real Bermudian locations. Unfortunately, the inspirations don't necessarily meet our needs. Romer Treece's lighthouse, for example, was modeled on a real one on Bermuda's St. David's Island. But the original is neither isolated enough to serve as our reclusive hero's home, nor likely to be cheerily sacrificed by its real owners for the story's climax, when we'll have to blow it up. We'll have to build a complete lighthouse for Treece; not only a detailed interior set, but a perfect façade as well on some as-yet-unfound perfect location. And the real beach lift which inspired the novel's Orange Grove elevator turned out to be an unimpressive and long defunct structure that won't be of any use to us. We'll have to go into the elevator construction business, too.

All this will cost money—a lot of it. Bermuda is expensive, partly because it's a popular resort; partly because, as an island with virtually no agriculture or industry, most of its goods must be flown or shipped in. We'll have to bring huge amounts of equipment and material into the country ourselves, and the costs of maintaining a crew there for three months at the height of tourist season will be inflated. Nevertheless, the pros of Bermuda outweigh the cons—we will film *The Deep* here.

That is, if the Bermudians will let us.

Bermuda, a self-governing British colony, is a tiny place. Its population of approximately 56,000 people makes it smaller than several American towns and even a few universities. But it has enough government for a place ten times the size. Bermuda has a Governor, a Cabinet Premier, a Legislative Council, a House of Assembly, Ministries, Departments, Secretaries, and Directors *ad infinitum*. It's a benevolent bureaucracy —but a bureaucracy just the same. And charged with the duty of keeping peaceful, picturesque Bermuda peaceful and picturesque, the government takes its responsibilities very seriously indeed. Its overprotective attitude is not just passionate chauvinism (though that's part of it). Bermuda's industry is tourism. Period. Bermuda's officials want to make very sure that any film we make doesn't jeopardize the image on which that thriving tourist trade depends.

And so we have begun our dealings with the island's government, through its Department of Tourism, starting the moment we returned to California. Our reasonably friendly first meeting with the heads of the Department was followed up with the book galleys. Trouble was not far behind. Bermudians are not too crazy about *The Deep*'s portrayal of their country. The story certainly features possibilities for showcasing Bermuda's charms. But it also refers to the embarrassments of racial strife, malevolent practitioners of voodoo, a healthy underground drug trade, and an indifferent police force, not to mention sharks and vicious eels.

To be fair, such things are really more typical of the Caribbean islands than they are of Bermuda, which, after some earlier spurts of unrest, has become rather placid in recent years. However, if we paint everything too hunky-dory, we won't have a story. So we have to negotiate the tricky line of cooperating to some extent with the government's wishes, while making it clear that we won't accept story censorship. We have carefully pointed out that wherever we end up filming, we'd establish the location of the story as Bermuda. And we have reminded them of the huge amounts of money we'd be pumping into their economy, something like five million dollars, much of it in areas that never see tourist dollars: the construction industry, local labor, and so on.

Well, that does sound good. But they want to see the script, and we don't have one! Although we've agreed to make the changes they demanded in the interest of accuracy, weeks have passed, and we still hadn't received word either way. We sent a recce to the Bahamas just in case, but we only became more convinced than ever that Bermuda was our first choice. Letters. Phone calls. Another recce to Bermuda, and more meetings.

At long last, the Bermudian officials have decided they like the "cut of our jib," and have given us permission to make our movie in their country—subject, of course, to various rules and regulations. The next step is to work our way through the dizzying array of departments before the location arrangements and work on our surface sets in Bermuda can begin full steam.

Now we have a whole separate phase of the production to engineer: the filming of *The Deep*'s numerous underwater scenes. Before anything else can be determined, we have to locate the underwater experts so crucial to our project. Two of them have been recommended straight from the source, Peter Benchley.

Romer Treece, the arrogant and authoritative treasure diver Benchley created for *The Deep,* is not total fabrication. He's inspired by a good friend of Benchley's who's a fascinating character in his own right. Teddy Tucker looks less like the hulking Indian described in the novel than like a roly-poly Bermudian Teddy Bear, but his exploits as a diver and shipwreck expert easily rival Romer Treece's. They're the stuff of real-life legend. Teddy and his attractive wife, Edna, live in a big old house filled with museum-value artifacts and antiques. In one of our more exciting jaunts on our first location trip, we had met the legendary man who had inspired our story, and we managed to lure him back to *The Deep*—as a consultant on the film.

February 24

Another of Benchley's best friends is a man universally acknowledged as the dean of underwater cinematographers, Stan Waterman. Stan has been diving for over twenty years and filming in the deep for almost as long. He's worked in just about every body of water you can name, as well as a few you probably can't. Again the sensational shark feature, *Blue Water, White Death,* will contribute talent to our venture, as it is one among dozens of award-winning documentaries and television films to Stan's credit. I just recently flew east to meet with Stan and Yates, fully expecting some grizzled old man of the sea. Instead, I found myself eating steamed clams at New York City's Plaza Hotel with one of the most urbane, charming, elegant gentlemen I've ever met. Stan was very enthusiastic about the chance to work on what could, with luck, become the definitive underwater feature film. We're delighted to welcome this brilliant and eminently likeable fellow aboard.

Columbia Vice President John Vietch suggested Al Giddings for the next member of *The Deep*'s underwater production team. Al is larger than life, a real Renaissance man of the deep. He looks like a burly linebacker who'd make a great drinking partner. That he is not just brawn is evidenced by his achievements as an underwater film director and producer whose work on award-winning projects like *Shark's Treasure, The Mystery of the Andrea Doria,* and numerous underwater films have won him tremendous acclaim. Moreover, Al's underwater still photography is unsurpassed in technical perfection; he is also a maverick designer of underwater camera equipment, the president of his own filmmaking company, Sea Films, Inc., and the originator, owner, and operator of a unique 221–foot floating film studio, the research vessel *Eagle*.

Between Giddings and Waterman and their fantastic expertise and complementary personalities, *The Deep* can ask for no better. In fact, the two have known each other well for years, but no film before *The Deep* has ever been big enough to warrant hiring them both. They welcomed the chance to work side by side.

February 27

Al has flown down from San Francisco for our first meeting, and Peter explained what we have in mind: a film richer in underwater visuals than has ever been done before. The majesty and terror of the deep, portrayed in exquisite detail and jewel-like color. Everything from close-ups of golden treasure gleaming in underwater sand drifts to panoramic vistas of a huge shipwreck sprawled across the ocean floor. In other words, all the spectacular 35mm Panavision visuals which film viewers have come to expect from feature films shot on land—underwater.

"It sounds terrific," Al agreed. "There's a small problem, though. The camera equipment you need to accomplish all that doesn't exist."

It doesn't exist??

What *does* exist is exactly one underwater 35mm Panavision camera, a souvenir from the 1950's. This warhorse has a parallax viewing system, which diverts the image through a series of internal reflectors, giving a cameraman the shudders because he can't look directly at what he's filming. Panavision #17 takes one standard length lens (thus no telephoto or wide-angle), it can run only at standard speed, and it has almost no range of aperture or shutter speed—together, these factors control the light that falls onto the film and how the image is focused. The camera has none of the modern fittings which help counteract the optical hijinx involved in filming in water. To top it off, #17 is really clunky—over 150 pounds—and requires two men to move it.

For Yates to tell *The Deep*'s intricate underwater story with this monster would be something like trying to sculpt the Pieta with a sledgehammer. Not even Al Giddings and Stan Waterman could possibly get results that are anywhere near our hopes with this camera.

To make *The Deep* at all, then, completely new camera systems will have to be built. There's just one small question: are these hypothetical technical advances even within the realm of possibility?

Al thinks so. Certainly if anyone can design and build them for us, he can. It's a huge gamble. The start of filming is merely three months away, and suddenly the whole production hinges on one huge, widescreen "IF." But there's no turning back now. So, to the tune of tens of thousands of dollars, we'll give Al our blessings, cross as many fingers as we can spare, and continue to pour thousands of dollars and hours into *The Deep*. We can't even be sure we'll be able to get it onto film when the moment of truth comes!

As if designing the brand new underwater camera systems on which the success of the entire film depends isn't enough, we've asked Al to find us an underwater location for their use, too. It's time to select a shipwreck to act as our story's *Goliath,* the morphine-laden World War II wreck onto which our characters unwittingly stumble, tripping the plot mechanism.

There are untold thousands of shipwrecks in the world. But *our* shipwreck has a lot of qualifications to fill. It has to be lying in very clear, relatively shallow (100 feet or less) water, close to hotel and diving facilities. It has to be fantastic-looking, cavernous, and mysterious, with a huge, intact hull section. It has to be perfect.

This is a problem we'll continually face. Reality is not always consistent with expectation and belief. Most people imagine a sunken ship lying quietly on her keel, clearly discernible, with deck chairs all in place and waiters with hot breakfasts frozen in time. Bermuda alone is the site of several hundred shipwrecks in shallow water, the hapless victims over the centuries of her attractive location between the Old World and the New, and her deadly reefs. But marine organisms and human hands have reduced most of these to little more than large piles of rubble—a fate most wrecks at that depth suffer in time.

March 8

And Bermuda waters just aren't consistently clear enough for the wide range of underwater filming we have to do. That means we'll have to do our underwater scenes in a whole separate location.

Working from his own memory and the suggestions of other divers, Al went on a whirlwind two-week tour of several possible sites throughout Florida, Mexico, and the Carribbean. He came back exhausted, but convinced he'd found our baby: a wreck called the *Balboa* lying off Grand Cayman Islands in the Caribbean. He and Yates went off to examine it. But by then Stan Waterman had heard about another wreck, rumored to be so fantastic that we urged them to go look at it. Al and Peter obligingly hopped on a jet and went to see the wreck of the *Rhone,* in the British Virgin Islands.

Well, it's put the *Balboa* to shame: the *R.M.S. Rhone* is a huge wreck lying in pellucid waters, forty minutes to sea from a luxurious beachside hotel complex. Even Al, who has been in and out of shipwrecks all over the world for most of his adult life, was bowled over. "That's our *Goliath*," Yates announced when he came back today. We'll begin right away to make the necessary arrangements.

We have a long way to go and we're running horrendously behind schedule and over budget, but the excitement is overwhelming with each piece of the puzzle we're able to solve. In spite of frequent attacks of panic, I am really up to my ears in making a major motion picture!

2
IN OVER OUR HEADS?

"Film under the ocean with actors?" The Columbia brass cried today. "Are you crazy?"

Although we've found a terrific shipwreck for our underwater sequences, we haven't exactly figured out just how we're going to film those scenes yet. Our desire for authenticity is causing a slight disagreement with Columbia executives.

Ocean filming is just about the biggest bugaboo in Hollywood. For decades, Hollywood has kept its oceans right where it keeps lightning, thunder, the Left Bank of Paris and old New York City: on the back lot. Most underwater filming is done in a tank—an unlikely blend of sound stage and aquarium, about forty feet wide and fifteen feet deep, with portholes in the side through which a land camera can film without getting so much as a lens cap wet. The tank is filled with models or props as needed, and the water is laced with chicken parts or milk to make it look as cloudy as the real briny deep. Actors are lowered in, head and torso shots photographed at all angles to be punched in to scenes performed later by doubles, and that's that.

The tanks have served Hollywood well for years, and I won't disillusion you with a list of all the terrific film moments you've seen on screen that were tank miracles. But for *The Deep*—for the number and the complexity of scenes we have to do underwater, and for the credibility and excitement they absolutely demand if the film is going to come off at all—a tank just will not do.

The trouble is that even controlled tank shooting

has a fair share of agonies. Water will be water where-
ever it is, wet, messy, and unpredictable. And the
problems involved in our proposed ocean filming are
enough to give any conscientious studio executive reason for dropping the whole thing then and there. Not
only do we have nearly enough scenes on the ocean's
surface to scuttle film budgets as monumental as those of
Jaws and *Lucky Lady*. Yates was going to have to shoot
complicated dramatic action sequences all around a
wreck lying in eighty–plus feet of water, and actually
have to go deep *inside* the wreck for numerous key
scenes, an exercise in acute danger and galloping
claustrophobia.

Nobody really believes that we'll actually get Hollywood stars to risk life and limb on a remote Caribbean shipwreck—not even for their names in lights
and a percentage of the film's profits. Between that
and the logistical terrors of filming in the deep, the
Columbia executives are naturally determined that we
somehow make do in a tank. But Yates is just as resolved to avoid the fatal artificiality of a tank at all
costs. It's a Mexican standoff.

We may be saved!

Tony Masters, the brilliant British production designer Yates hired, has proposed the ideal compromise. Tony masterminded the total production design
of that incredible film milestone, *2,001*. Today, in
the middle of the most heated debate yet, we realized
that if Stanley Kubrick could listen to what Tony had
to say for the five years it took to conceive and make
that epic, we could afford to listen very carefully indeed for the next five minutes. It was priceless.

To do all of our underwater filming in the ocean
just wasn't viable, Yates pointed out. The FilmWorks
contingent reluctantly nodded. To do any of our underwater filming in a tank just wasn't palatable. The
Columbia contingent bit their nails. "So," Tony declared, "when we can't go into the ocean, let's bring
the ocean to us!" In other words, build our own con-
trollable underwater set right on location, using all
the visual elements that the real ocean offers: real sea

water, real fish and sea life . . . a total, absolutely authentic underwater environment, the biggest such undertaking in the world. That way, we could do all the key establishing exterior scenes on the actual wreck of the *Rhone* in the Caribbean off the British Virgin Islands, but do the intricate scenes which had to take place inside the shipwreck on an underwater set painstakingly built to look just like the real thing.

Everyone sat up in their seats cautiously. It sounded good. But Tony wasn't finished, and his final brainstorm turned out to be the best one yet. If we built a set of the *Rhone* interior—our *Goliath*—we could also include the *Grifon,* the treasure-laden sunken Spanish galleon which, in the story, lies beneath the World War II wreck. This could take the form of a hidden chamber long sealed off by sand and rock. The underwater artillery explosion that David accidentally causes could then be the force that knocks those rocks ajar, causing a mini-landslide that would dramatically propel him into the grave of the *Grifon*.

Well, that was one terrific idea, since even in the book the exact relation of the *Goliath* to the *Grifon* was frustratingly fuzzy and hard to visualize. On film, one of our characters poking around and coming up with an old pewter spoon wouldn't exactly inspire the audience to cheers. But a cataclysmic tumble into a spooky, centuries-old hidden chamber—*that* just might.

Yates and I love it. Columbia loves it and gives the official go-ahead. Peter Benchley loves it and is writing it into the first draft screenplay he's working on. Tony, who will oversee the production of the set, has begun making preliminary sketches. The word BUS—an anagram for the world's Biggest Underwater Set—is cropping up on inter-office memos with increasing frequency. And increasing panic. It has all too quickly become evident that conceiving, designing, and building this inspiration will be one mammoth job.

At this point we have imported more expertise. Jack Maxstead, an outstanding British art director who has worked with Tony on several films over the past twelve years (*Papillon, The Adventurers*) and won the

Academy Award for *Nicholas and Alexandra,* came running. The two of them hustled back to Bermuda and, from precious few possibilities, chose the now-deserted site of the old LeFevre yellow-fever hospital for our set. But even before this one problem was solved, they had another on their hands.

Back in Los Angeles, Masters and Maxstead had begun drawing up plans and realized they needed help in creating the set and the total biological environment it would have to sustain. So Tony and Jack called in Kym Murphy, a marine biologist and consulting engineer who had played a vital part in the creation of San Diego's Sea World, the biggest seaquarium in the world. Kym in turn drafted Carlos Machado, a brilliant young designer of animal habitats for zoos and seaquariums who had also been one of Sea World's prime movers. Carlos will conceive, artificially create, and install the numerous corals, sponges, and other sea vegetation we'll need for our set. Though it's to be a precise duplicate of their natural environment, we've discovered that the delicate Real McCoy can't survive the trip.

Tony has brought in another art director from England, Terry Ackland-Snow, to take full charge of the set's execution. Terry took a diving course back home to be abreast of his duties, and is now scurrying back and forth between Bermuda and BVI to make sure that the set about to be built will match the *Rhone* in every way.

As for Peter Yates and me, we're leaving the BUS in these talented people's hands, saying several fervent prayers, and turning our attention to the multitude of other preproduction problems screaming for attention.

By now hundreds of thousands of dollars have been sunk into a production that depends on cameras which don't exist, to be used on a set the likes of which have never before been built. I guess it's only logical that with all this going on, we also have to build a moray eel.

In the novel, a twelve-foot-long green moray eel (dubbed "Percy" by Treece) lives in a cave near the

Goliath. In the screenplay, the cave, for reasons of simplicity, had been omitted. But the eel is still very much alive in our version of *The Deep,* now residing in the wreck itself. And Percy still figures dramatically in the story's climax, when he decides the outcome of a violent underwater struggle between Cloche and Treece by emerging suddenly from his hole, chomping down on Cloche's head, and tearing the villain to a grisly death.

Now, it was one thing for Peter Benchley to sit at his typewriter and write that scene, and quite another thing for us to make it happen before the cameras. Not one twelve-foot moray eel that would bite an actor's head off on cue answered our casting call. We'll have to build ourselves a Percy who will do our bidding, and biting, take after take after take. And we'll have to build him very well indeed. When you're creating a monster for the movies, it's either spectacular or laughable . . . there's no in-between.

March 20

Hollywood has manufactured monsters of every description, of course, but no one has ever constructed a moray eel before. In Walter Stones' case, it's probably simply because no one had ever asked him to. Walter is a wiry, energetic, forty-nine-year veteran of the film industry, most recently at Disney Studios, where he created the dazzling special effects both in films like *Mary Poppins* and in some of the most sensational attractions at Disneyland. Walter had been peacefully retired from his adventures, but he agreed to go back to his blueprints and brainstorms for the sake of *The Deep.* Walter called in his partner Charlie Spurgeon, another industry old-timer who'd been doing special effects work for movies before they even called it special effects, and together they've begun to build our eel.

Just how dangerous is the moray eel? No doubt the moray's looks alone could ensure its reputation as a real sea monster, right in a league with the shark and the barracuda. Morays, which are actually sea snakes, may range from two to as much as fifteen feet in length, and six- to eight-footers are not uncommon.

Whatever its size, the moray eel has some unpleasant features which can make a brush with even a small specimen harrowing, and an encounter with a large one —like our own twelve-footer—a full-fledged nightmare.

The moray eel gazes out of its watery world through beady cold eyes planted in a singularly ugly head. Its jaws are chilling to behold, studded with several ragged rows of vicious fangs reaching all the way back and around into the creature's throat. Those jaws are capable of fearsome damage, especially since the moray is reluctant to let go once it's clamped down on something—or someone. If those jaws don't finish you off, the lack of air from being trapped in their painful grasp below the water's surface certainly would.

Reports have documented tales of eight-foot eels which have been speared by divers twisting around, tearing the long darts out of their bodies, and quickly, angrily slithering up the steel spears right toward their human tormentors. The truth is that an experienced diver is not automatically in danger of his life when he is in the vicinity of a large moray eel. The animal resides in a lair, inside which it anchors itself by twisting its tail end around a rock or some other point of leverage. It can thus lunge out of its cave or hole with such lightning speed and accuracy when prey swims by that the victim has little chance for escape. To avoid moray attacks you simply avoid poking around dark holes where a moray lurking inside can mistake your head for a fish or your hand for an octopus, its favorite dinner. It's a lesson David and Gail, the young heroes of *The Deep,* both have to learn the hard way.

Walter and Charlie decided to capitalize on the moray's natural tendency to burrow into its own home, revealing only the front half of its torso when it darts out to snatch its prey. Our eel will be able to be controlled from the rear by special effects divers stationed in his hole, offscreen. With their help, "Percy" will be able to move from side to side, up and down, forward and back, to breathe through his mouth, and in general, to move just like a real moray. He will also be able to bite Cloche's head off.

You must realize that at this time, we don't even know who's going to play our villain. But we do feel safe in assuming that any actor we cast is not going to be terribly eager to be decapitated underwater by a twelve-foot mechanical eel with sharp metal teeth. Our gory climax can only be shown in full detail—tooth marks and all—on a convincing dummy head of whatever actor we cast. And for Percy's scenes with a real man, he'd better have soft rubber teeth so that no real harm will be done.

Walter and Charlie have suggested that we build two separate eels, one with hard teeth, one with soft, rather than one eel with two sets of portable teeth. The second will be far cheaper than the first, since the molds and hydraulics will already be designed. The cost will quickly be regained in time saved by not having to switch the teeth back and forth. Besides, having a back-up Percy certainly won't hurt matters.

Before Percy's finest hour, though, we'll have to introduce him to our audience in a memorable way. For that purpose, two frightening earlier eel encounters have been written into the script. One of these will require a perfectly lifelike, full-size, twelve-foot Percy which will be pulled quickly past the cameras, creating (we hope) the effect of a real eel whipping rapidly across the screen. This non-hydraulic "rigid" Percy doesn't have to do anything but look mean and real.

But his mechanical brothers, Percy I and II, can't just be pretty faces—they have to act. So Charlie and Walter are designing a hydraulic system that is as compact and efficient as possible. They've also been looking for a sculptor.

Our sculptor will have to make a full-scale sculpture of a moray eel, accurate down to the last detail, from which a series of molds will be made, first in plaster, then in fiberglass. Only then can Percy's body be created in lifelike rubber latex skin, to be fitted with the intricate system that will make him come to life.

March 27

But Walter and Charlie couldn't find a sculptor. Every sculptor in town seemed to be busy on the Dino

DeLaurentiis remake of *King Kong*—they were sculpting big gorillas, little gorillas, gorrilla hands, gorilla faces, you name it. Finally, in desperation, they called the 20th Century-Fox staff shop, and happened to hook up with Madeleine McLaughlin, a veteran Hollywood sculptress who was being laid off due to budget cuts that very night. Would she be interested in sculpting a twelve-foot moray eel? She would indeed.

And so Madeleine began sculpting Percy, working from key film footage and photographs of a real green moray eel that we'd discovered in Bermuda. We'll be making this particular live eel a star in some back-up shots in days to come.

Naturally, we've all been dying to see our monster. As soon as Madeleine completed her sculpture, several of us raced over to Fox to see it. We were horrified to see something that looked like a large sea horse. It just didn't look like a moray—or, rather, what we thought a moray should look like. "Make his chin smaller!" "How about lowering his eyebrows?" "Let's try smoothing down his nostrils!" Madeleine rushed around trying to do as we pleaded. Finally we ran out of things to say, and Percy looked worse than ever; clearly we were no help.

Back to the photographs and films and more agonizing over just what constituted a properly photogenic moray eel. Today, Kym Murphy visited the sculpture and saw the trouble right away: its skin was too wrinkled because Madeleine had relied mostly on pictures of a dead, and thus dehydrated, eel. Again Madeleine took up her sculpting tools, and already Percy has begun to take shape.

Back in Walter Stones' Culver City home workroom, which has now become our Percy factory, our boys are hard at work on Percy's moving parts. Designing a mechanical monster to work underwater is ticklish business, not only because land and water performance are two completely different things, but also because immersing certain metals in salt water is like giving them an acid bath. So Walter and Charlie have designed Percy's parts in stainless steel or bronze, both impervious to rust. They came up with the idea of attaching a zinc ball to Percy's rear, a technique often used on boat propellers, to ward off the damaging chemical process of electrolysis. They have created what Walter proudly called a "Geneva watch movement" in Percy's head which will allow him to breathe or attack, or to do both at the same time. Incorporating these and other foxy ploys, Charlie and Walter built a two-foot model of Percy, using strings and piano wire instead of steel rods and cables.

But Percy still isn't ready for the big time yet: the mini-eel's movements are klutzy and abrupt, not at all the smooth, fluid motions we'll need. Back to the old drawing board. Walter and Charlie added long plastic strips along the length of Percy's body to give him a sinuous motion that his stainless steel ribs could not. So it goes, step by step, with Peter Lake monitoring progress in periodic trips to Percyville.

April 5

It's clear by this time that Percy's attack on Cloche is going to be hell to shoot. In fact, none of Percy's scenes promise to be anything less than full-fledged grief. Our only hope is to plan them as carefully as possible. Peter Yates' storyboards—sketches of shots for each scene drawn by Tony Masters—now fill a mass of pages thicker than the script itself. This accomplished, we merely have to try everything we can imagine to implement them. And the implementation also means working with our live seven-foot eel to establish the reality of the creature on film. But how to cut it together convincingly with the mechanical twelve-foot eel material? The real thing is half the size of his hydraulic twin. Unless . . . we show the real thing— with half-size men that make *it* look twelve feet long!

No, that doesn't mean casting midgets as Treece and Cloche. It does mean *building* three-foot replicas of our as-yet uncast stars, to appear in certain very carefully set up quick shots with the real moray. Thus preliminary work on our "munchkins" has begun—at a cost of tens of thousands of dollars, pending casting and costuming.

We're none too sure that any of these concepts will

actually work, but we are in no position to discard any possibility. And this is just preproduction!

If not exactly bliss, our relative ignorance is enough to keep the wheels turning, even through another crisis of hefty proportions. Eels aren't the only sea monsters sinking their fangs into our schedule, budget, and sanity: we have shark troubles, too.

Peter Benchley's name, of course, is synonymous with sharks. While his second novel has plenty of other things going on, it also features several frightening run-ins with the creatures. We have no intention of making a shark movie; in fact, if we're going to use sharks at all, we'll have to use them in a truly spectacular way to avoid comparison with you-know-what. So we've decided to combine the several shark incidents in the book into what promises to be one terrifying sequence.

There's just one problem: the type of sharks we need don't exist in great quantity in Bermuda. That's nice for the Bermudians, but it spells disaster for us. Al and Stan know of only one surefire way to make our shark scene really work: send the underwater team to the shark-infested waters of the Great Barrier Reefs of Australia.

Omigod. Bermuda . . . British Virgin Islands . . . now Australia too? Are we making a feature film or a multi-million dollar travelogue on remote British island territories? Meeting after meeting has been held about this controversial proposal. Al and Stan are adamant about Australia's being the place to get the most "shark value" for the money. Certainly, unless we can gather the necessary sharks in Bermudian waters once we begin filming, there's no alternative. It's time, I'm afraid, to figure a trip to Australia into our budget and schedule—but I'm hoping against hope that it won't have to be made.

Usually, in film planning, you try to "break the back" of the film—to get the worst part over with first. But in *The Deep,* everything promises to be the worst. Underwater photography is only the beginning of our problems. There are also the numerous mechanical special effects, both on land and in water—explosions, crashes, monsters, phony blood, everything physical which has to be engineered to get a certain effect on screen; and a boggling number of optical special effects—the sophisticated processes that create effects in the camera and in the lab.

But our biggest headache at this point is scheduling. Everywhere Yates and the team will turn, they'll be at the mercy of weather. Late summer hurricanes are a real possibility in both BVI and Bermuda, and a crew out on a boat 300 miles off the North Australian coast will be all too vulnerable to any kind of storm. Almost every single underwater scene is to be shot at two, and at least one at all three locations, and everything shot has to work with everything else.

We've decided to begin in BVI for a month of underwater on-location filming. There, we'll work with doubles if necessary, and hopefully get our stars down into the ocean at least for some key establishing shots. The production will then move on to Bermuda for three months, where we'll accomplish the majority of our underwater filming in the controlled environment of our underwater set; we'll also have the cushion of the ocean around Bermuda for any additional sea filming necessary. After the main underwater set filming has been completed, our underwater team will go on to Australia while the land unit continues to shoot all of our land and surface ocean scenes in Bermuda. Then the underwater team will return with their shark footage to finish work in the underwater set, now re-dressed for the optical special effects work still necessary to complete the film.

April 16

Not surprisingly, the Columbia executives are by now climbing the executive suite walls over *The Deep*. The estimated budget has soared to $8 million, and it promises to be a long, grueling shoot. The book itself has not even been published yet, and to a large extent the success of the movie will depend on the success of the book. Most unbelievable of all our crises, however, is the fact that we still do not have an approved screenplay.

The screenplay is turning out to be murder to write. Peter Benchley had to rework much of the story not only for visual artistic reasons, but to prevent the actual film production from becoming a nightmare of logistics. Much of it is in fairly good shape, but as a whole Columbia feels it still needs work. Benchley has by now plowed his way through two complete drafts. He's worked like the devil and come up with some inspired improvements in his own material. But it has gradually become apparent that it's time for some fresh input. It was a difficult conclusion to reach, so Yates and I breathed a sigh of relief when Peter confronted the topic first. Maybe, he said delicately, we've gone as far as we can together, and it's time to call in another writer. His contribution has been fantastic, and this is yet another example of his professionalism.

April 23

So Tracy Keenan Wynn, another scion of a famous entertainment family (he's the son of actor Keenan Wynn, and grandson of the immortal Ed Wynn) and a successful young screenwriter (*The Longest Yard, Autobiography of Miss Jane Pittman, The Glass House*) has been brought in. Tracy brought a completely new point of view to the material and, with it, some fascinating new changes. But the script is still being furiously reworked and time to start assembling a cast for *The Deep* is growing short.

It's perfect timing. Just as we're fretting and sweating over the screenplay, a wonderful thing has happened: the novel has been published. It's a much needed shot in the arm.

Favorable reviews are pouring in. From the *Los Angeles Times. The New York Times Book Review. The Washington Post. National Observer.* "Benchley is a master!" "A book you can't put down!" "An exciting yarn!" The consensus is that *The Deep,* far from being a poor relation of *Jaws,* is in many ways better than its predecessor! The book is showing up in book clubs and in magazine serializations. First published in London, it quickly zoomed to the top of England's best-seller lists and is now appearing on all the American lists.

We have a hit on our hands!

3
STAR BAIT

The early skeptics at Columbia are optimistic, and the early optimists are ecstatic. For the moment placated out of its script worries, the studio has given official go-ahead to start putting together a cast. And not a moment too soon: the start of filming is only about two months away! We still don't have a script with which to woo potential stars. But in addition to the always-potent *Jaws* recommendation, we now have a best-selling book and the absolute guarantee that, come hell or high water, this picture is a high-profile "go." All these things help, but without a screenplay and on such short notice, we're still having to do some fancy dancing to get the cast we want.

When you're making a big-budget film, your instinct is to go for "big" names. They may cost a fortune, but it's standard industry wisdom that they more than make up for their expense at the box office. This is not always true: Almost every superstar has been cast in one colossal turkey that even his or her famous name couldn't save, but for the most part, the theory holds for American movie-goers. And when you're dealing with exhibitors and foreign distributors, the presence or absence of big names often makes or breaks the bargain. Our problem is all too obvious— no major actors or actresses have ever dived before! No cameras, no underwater set, no actor-divers—this is utterly ridiculous. Still we're pressing on.

We began casting meetings for *The Deep* by mulling over actors like Charlton Heston, Burt Lancaster, Robert Mitchum, and Sean Connery for the role of Romer Treece. But Yates and I thought Robert Shaw would be perfect. He appeared sensationally in the last Benchley epic, *Jaws,* a fact which discouraged some Columbia people who felt that our audiences will think *The Deep* is a sequel.

But Romer Treece is a completely different character from Quint the shark hunter, and Shaw's career proves him capable of handling any character. Through the incredible diversity of Shaw's screen personalities, an arrogance and power is transmitted which would make him perfect for Romer Treece. We're going to give it a shot.

Shaw, always a critically acclaimed performer, has grown from his beginnings as "that great English actor Robert Whatzisname" to a full-fledged film star who commands an enormous salary and is often booked up a year in advance. He can pick and choose his projects. As the author of several prestigious books and plays, including *The Man In The Glass Booth* and *The Hiding Place,* Shaw is very concerned about the literary quality of any project he takes on. In fact, Robert Shaw has never committed to a film without a screenplay, and he doesn't read one without a firm offer. We have neither.

Yet Robert agreed to read the book, essentially through the good offices of John Gaines, his agent. Today Yates and I sat down with Shaw and his secretary Virginia Jansen in his Beverly Hills home and began my crusade to convince this imperious, magnetic man why he should be in our movie. His character, already strong in the book, will be the dominant force in the film. The story is being woven into a tight, compelling screenplay even as we speak . . . On and on we rattled nervously. When we were finished, Robert sat quietly for several minutes, peering at us with those ice blue eyes, and then leaned forward. "I'll do it! I don't know why . . . it just has the right smell.

"So be sure to deliver a good script or you'll have one unhappy actor on your hands!"

Our first major role is cast—and with a consummate actor who is willing to learn how to dive! Now we have to find our David . . . one who won't be overwhelmed by Shaw's strong screen personality.

The character of David Sanders has undergone a big transition from book to script. Instead of the skeptical, self-protective hero of the novel, the film's David is to be a restless, energetic young man looking for fame, fortune, and above all, identity. That will be his motivation for getting involved in the dangerous quest for treasure, a quest which, much through Benchley's own efforts, now stands out in bolder relief than it did in the book. Finally, after his harrowing adventures, David learns to look within himself for the key to his existence, which, symbolically, has been in his hands from the beginning in the form of an old Spanish medallion, its fabulous secret embedded in a lump of coal.

In Hollywood casting meetings, you leave no stone unturned. You try to think of everyone likely, however remote, and then begin the weeding process. And we've thought of everyone, all right. Our casting directors Mike Fenton and Jane Feinberg have pored over box office stars of proven appeal like Ryan O'Neal and Jeff Bridges, rising young stars like Paul LeMat and Jan Michael Vincent, offbeat suggestions like Richard Benjamin and television stars like David Groh. Even comic Chevy Chase's name has wound up on a list or two.

And then someone asked, "How about Nick Nolte?"

Nick Nolte is the hottest thing on television. After years of acting regularly but in relative anonymity on stage and television, Nolte has hit big with his intense portrayal of the "bad" brother, Tom Jordache, in the ABC anthology series *Rich Man, Poor Man*. He's received an Emmy nomination and has received so much acclaim that the show's producers, having carelessly killed off his character, are frantically trying to bring Nick back for the sequel by having him play his own son!

But Nolte isn't interested. He's beseiged with movie offers, and he's picking them over very carefully. After viewing the show and meeting with him, I think

Nick would make a sensational David Sanders. Nick, however, isn't interested. And Columbia isn't convinced that a television star making his first feature will lend enough support to an eight-million-dollar film.

So I've begun a naughty little game of playing both ends against the middle, trying to persuade Columbia to consider Nick and at the same time to entice Nick into the project. Meanwhile, Peter Yates has decided that he doesn't think Nick is "right for the role." And Nick, after reading the book, has definitely decided against doing *The Deep;* he just doesn't care for the character of David Sanders. I've urged Nick to reconsider; after all, we *are* rewriting his character substantially. Nolte has at least agreed to meet with Yates and me.

Yesterday, I walked into a conference that could not have started on shakier ground if we'd held it on the San Andreas fault. Here was an actor that the studio didn't want, sitting down to discuss a part he'd already rejected, with a filmmaker who'd decided he wasn't right for the role anyway! Nick immediately sensed that Yates wasn't too thrilled with him for the character. But as they talked, Nick became intrigued with the changing character and with the challenge of working underwater, and Yates became intrigued with Nick. Finally, after two hours, Yates reached across the table to Nick and said, "You're the man for me," knocking Nick for a loop. Last night, his manager Mimi Weber and his agent Lou Pitt called to say that Nick had decided to do *The Deep* and was waiting for me to make a firm offer. Now I had to somehow quickly convince the studio to go with Nick. And if Columbia wouldn't back my position, I was in hot water.

In Hollywood, important decisions are frequently made, not in boardrooms, but in restaurants, living rooms, backyards, hot tubs, wherever industry members congregate and socialize. This time it was a cocktail party at Sue Mengers' house. Sue is a dynamic super-agent who represents some of the biggest names in Hollywood, so when she holds a party you can bet the "A" list—the important film industry people—will be there. In this case, the one person most important to *The Deep* happened to be in attendance—David Begelman, President of Columbia Pictures.

Well, David got it from all sides last night, as word of Nolte in *The Deep* percolated throughout the party. Several people—including Sue Mengers herself and powerful columnist Rex Reed—approved wholeheartedly of his being cast, and they let David know it. David arrived at the office this morning to learn that V.P. Stanley Jaffe had also gotten the pro-Nolte treatment from another influential Hollywood personality, Rona Barrett. If it had been a conspiracy, it couldn't have been timed so perfectly or worked so well. Columbia has approved Nick for the role, and a deal has been made.

May 2

It's time to cast the role which in many ways will be the key to the film's success. Gail is the film's only female character and the center of its emotional triangle. She's got to be a good actress, an appropriate foil for the intense screen personalities of Shaw and Nolte. And since she's the only woman the audience will see for nigh on two hours, usually in a bathing suit, she should be one terrific-looking lady.

Every actress you can imagine has been mentioned. The list included obvious leading ladies like Candice Bergen and Katherine Ross, European stars like Samantha Eggar and Charlotte Rampling, up-and-coming starlets like Susan Blakely and Christina Raines. My own first choice for Gail is Jacqueline Bisset.

Jackie has made a splash in dozens of films both in America and abroad, notably, *Bullitt, Airport, Day for Night,* and *Murder on the Orient Express.* She's a big star in many foreign countries, an important asset in foreign distribution. And I feel sure that the chemistry between Jackie and Nick would be explosive. Her dark hair, his blonde looks; her elegant sophistication, his diamond-in-the-rough quality. Together, they'd invest the relationship of David and Gail with some much-needed intrigue and tension.

But Columbia had other ideas. They'd decided it would be a terrific idea to launch a talent search for an unknown beauty to play Gail. It would make for great publicity, they figured, and it was always possible that we just might discover a new female sensation.

So the call was issued. The word spread fast, and we were soon bombarded. Not only was each theatrical agency in town sending us every starving starlet and ambitious model on their rosters, there were also hundreds of phone calls from people whose girl friend, or secretary, or sister, or babysitter was perfect for the part. Pictures of girls in bathing suits poured in from all over the country, accompanied by letters assuring us that they were right for the role because they could swim, or they loved to drink water, or other similarly formidable qualifications. One enterprising young Hollywood hopeful even crawled into my car one evening and waited there all night to pounce on me with a request for an audition when I unwittingly opened the door hours later! There were wall-to-wall appointments with sweet young things, and wall-to-wall readings with an amazingly obliging Nick Nolte.

But even with such titillating breaks in the routine, the whole experiment soon became a crashing bore. Our talent search was revealing precious little talent amid all that rosy flesh and all those retroussé noses. The girls just didn't have "it"—star quality, charisma, presence, call it what you will. We still wanted Jacqueline Bisset for Gail, more than ever. And now we were afraid we'd lost her.

May 8

Because by this time, Jackie was a bit fed up with Columbia's wishy-washy attitude toward casting her. And their insistence on someone who "looked like Ursula Andress in a bikini" exasperated Jackie, who thought the comparison silly and unfair. She was right on the first score, but overly modest on the second. A meeting with Jackie in London finally convinced Columbia's Stan Jaffe that Jacqueline Bisset was our Gail. There was plenty of jockeying back and forth. At long last, Jackie has given her tentative consent, on the condition that she'll be given second position billing after

Robert Shaw, something which Nick has already been granted.

Nick refused to budge . . . that is, until he met Jackie. Last evening we went to her house, along with her agent Ben Benjamin. Jackie's boyfriend, French garment manufacturer Victor Drai, was there, and he was eyeing Nick like Percy the Eel contemplating a possible meal. Tension was so thick you could have cut it with a knife. But things finally relaxed and everyone began getting along splendidly. We went out for a bite to eat and discussed the project animatedly until one in the morning. The deal is made, the differences are ironed out, and Jacqueline Bisset is in.

The rest of the roles are falling into place. As Cloche, we've cast Lou Gossett, a charismatic black actor with a long list of credits in both features and television, including *Skin Game* and *Travels with My Aunt,* as well as the highly acclaimed television anthology *Roots.* As Treece's brother Kevin, Yates cast an Algonquin Indian actor named Robert Tessier, a muscular, forceful screen presence who's been most recently featured in *The Longest Yard* and *Hard Times.*

We had a thorny problem with the matter of Cloche's henchman. In the book, all the villains are black. In the film, a situation like that is bound to generate some unfavorable press. We played with the thought that Bob Tessier should play Cloche's righthand man, Slake, instead. But Bob was perfect as Kevin. Some other compromise would have to be made.

Our dilemma has been resolved within the script. Adam Coffin, Treece's old friend, is now in effect the film's white villain. Tracy Keenan Wynn hit on the idea that Coffin, out of resentment at Treece, ultimately joins forces with Cloche against him. All we have to do is to find an Adam Coffin that can convincingly make such a turnaround and take the audience with him. We've juggled names like Richard Widmark and Sterling Hayden, but we can't seem to pin this key role down. It's a glaring hole in our plans that continues to plague us.

It's now only ten days before filming is to begin, and acute panic has set in because Tracy Keenan Wynn's draft is still not where Columbia wants it. They persist that the dialogue is still not up to snuff, but the script has improved. The plot now ticks along briskly, and the underwater action has been storyboarded and neatly broken down in detail by Yates. This will become his and the underwater team's Bible in the months to come, although he and Masters continue to review it as the shooting date approaches. This is a boon for our harried production. The underwater scenes as storyboarded are at least close enough to what we want for us to begin our underwater work in the British Virgin Islands. We have to face the fact, though, that Columbia wants additional work on the script before it can be shown to anyone. Though we are unhappy Columbia wants another fresh hand in the writing.

But by now our cast is clamoring to see the script! We're doing what we've been doing for weeks: We stall them. "Oh, just another week, now." Our master plan is to actually get them all onto location before letting them see a copy of the unrevised screenplay —hardly an orthodox procedure, but we're desperate. However, it's become clear that, at least in the case of Bisset and Shaw, our little ploy is not going to work. With copious assurances that it's still being rewritten, we've given Jackie the latest draft and sent a copy to Shaw's home in Ireland, and we're praying that they'll still show up on location when they're supposed to.

By this time I'm about ready to start cutting out paper dolls, but Yates is keeping calm. He suggested that we bring Tom Mankiewicz, an excellent screenwriter, to the British Virgin Islands for about ten days of polishing. It sounds like a nice interlude for many a writer, but Tom is currently engrossed at Warners in a six-figure screenwriting deal which he'll have the chance to direct. He isn't exactly eager to go to BVI and break his back for ten days revising a script that he won't even get any credit for. But Tom's an old friend of Yates', and we, being in such a bind, did everything but get down on our knees and beg. How could a guy say no? Tom has finally relented—he'll come down to BVI next week.

So everything on *The Deep* is in a state of limbo as our BVI start date draws inexorably closer. The Film-Works office has assumed a frantic Keystone Kops tone in these final days of preproduction.

Take two examples out of the many. Costume designer Ron Talsky is in turmoil because our stars have been cast rather late in the game and the role of Adam Coffin is as yet unfilled. That isn't Ron's only problem —he has to design the underwater wear in such a way that it will keep our actors warm and breathing without swathing them in so much rubber and apparatus that they look less like marquee idols than like Martians. The delay in costuming has also affected the design of outfits for our "munchkins" of Treece and Cloche, which have to be perfect little representations of actors Shaw and Gosset in underwater gear, right down to perfect little facemasks and waterproof wristwatches. Another worry is that, through no fault of their own, Walter and Charlie are running into trouble on Percy the eel, and we'll be lucky if they manage to squeeze in a few vital water tests of the creatures before having to ship them out for the start of filming in Bermuda.

The whole purpose of preproduction is to prepare for production. While everyone concerned has worked valiantly, we still have so many loose ends dangling that I feel something very close to sheer terror—and it's the day before I leave for location. There's small comfort in having surmounted huge obstacles when you know all too well that the worst is yet ahead!

But there will be no turning back. *The Deep* is holding strong at number one on several best-seller lists and shows no signs of slipping, just as we'd hoped. And Columbia has lost all its ambivalence toward the project, supported it through preproduction, and is now all but breathing down our necks to actually get out there and make the damn movie.

So it's into *The Deep* for real.

4

THE BRITISH VIRGINS LIGHT UP

~~~~~~

We're probably the most exciting thing to hit the British Virgin Islands in the last several hundred years, which tells you as much about BVI as it does about *The Deep*. In the seventeenth and eighteenth centuries, the British Virgins were a favorite hangout for pirates. Renegades fanned out through the forty–odd sparsely inhabited little islands and watched for the treasure-loaded ships passing by on their way between the Old World and the New. What the reefs didn't finish off, these rascals did. Things were therefore pretty exciting in that corner of the Caribbean for awhile. Eventually, buccaneers were driven out by settlers, and the British Virgin Islands quieted down . . . that is, until we renegades arrived.

Not that they made it easy for us. Centuries have made the British Virgins scarcely more accessible than they were in the days of Captain Hook and Long John Silver. In spite of all those colored lines crisscrossing airline maps to impress you with all the places they go, none of them fly right to the British Virgins. So, while all the Virgin Islands are sublimely, serenely gorgeous, the British Virgins especially are so untouched that they make the hotel- and nightclub-studded U.S. Virgins look like urban blight in comparison. As one typical guidebook rhapsodizes, "The visitor to BVI will find them to be as far removed from the tensions and anxieties of modern life as possible . . ." Translation: "BVI might not be the end of the earth, but it'll do in a pinch."

July 3

Because shooting was to begin July 5, I made travel plans for my wife Lynda, daughters, Jodi, eight and Elizabeth, four, and myself to BVI for the Fourth of July weekend. The result was a trip that I'll match with anyone's travel horror story, anytime. With eighteen pieces of luggage we were bumped from one flight; a bomb scare shut the next flight down, which meant extra hours at the hot, crowded, and chaotic San Juan airport, a hellish place if ever there was one. Finally, we caught a bumpity old DC-3 flight which lurched over the water to BVI's Beef Island. The airport there (to use the term loosely) is really one chicken-ridden, dusty strip of macadam that's home to a handful of small DC-3's shuttling back and forth to San Juan. We then had to take a tramlike affair to Roadtown, the sleepy little capital of BVI. To get to our location base, Peter Island, from there meant a half-hour scenic boat ride that turned out to be a lunch-losing battle with a gray and choppy sea.

This ghoulish itinerary wasn't cooked up especially for me by some demented travel agent. Every single member of our team and every single piece of equipment had to make the same trip, though not everyone's travel time added up to twenty-four solid hours, which mine did. But, somehow, we've all made it to Peter Island and have regrouped on this tiny, dazzling, real-life incarnation of your basic fantasy tropical isle: colorful flowers, rich foliage, picturesque mountains, spectacular beaches, and so much moisture in the air that even the fans perspired.

Peter Island's one concession to modern times is the Peter Island Yacht Club, a beautiful new resort owned and operated by some cannily capitalistic Norwegians. The Club is actually a Scandinavian-style cottage colony, but from the water it looks more like a lonely little Indian settlement, the structures huddled together for company against the huge, empty landscape. Inside, though, we have all the conveniences. And since it's summer and therefore off-season, *The Deep* crew has successfully commandeered it, suiting our needs perfectly.

The bungalow into which my family moved on the far tip of the colony has already come to be known as "Guber Gulch." Director Peter Yates, his wife Virginia and son Toby, Jacqueline Bisset, and First Assistant Director Derek Cracknell will be stashed in the splendid hilltop estate called "Crow's Nest." Bob Wolfe, the amiable film editor Yates hired straight from his superb work on *All the President's Men*, has moved into a separate bungalow with all his editing paraphernalia so that he can begin assembling footage as it's shot. All the remaining cast and crew has burrowed into the multiple condominium-like shelters clustered around the main facility. One of the sitting rooms off the open-air lobby of the Club has been converted to our production office; with makeshift black-out curtains and projector, it doubles as a screening room for viewing rushes.

And that's just about it, folks. We're the extent of the action on Peter Island. It's the perfect setting to develop a royal case of island fever. Except for the views from our Yacht Club windows, the only scenery we'll be seeing for a solid month will be underwater. And other than hotel personnel, boaters, and stray restaurant guests, the only faces we'll be seeing will be each others'.

Symptoms of island fever, in fact, have started to appear even before filming begins. Yates and I gave a July 4th party on the beach to relax the crew and to get everyone in a good frame of mind. Well, the piña coladas and sultry air did their work. As it dawned on several members of our predominately male crew that they'd have virtually no one of the fairer sex to share this paradise with for the next four weeks, they drunkenly began vying for the attentions of the few females among us.

The booze may have managed to take the sheen off the crew's manners, but it didn't begin to relax my own pre-shoot shivers. During preproduction I'd gradually learned more and more about what underwater filming entailed. Now, in BVI, the problems seem more formidable than ever. Trying to get to sleep last night, the night before shooting began, I found myself counting those problems instead of sheep . . .

One: clear water. For clear water, you need sunlight, and the water must be calm. The slightest wind aboveboard can cause a chop in the water that makes it impossible to work. Ocean "wind"—the surge beneath the surface—is even worse. When the sea is tossing you and your equipment around like spare change, it's hard to get anything resembling control. The current also stirs up sand and sweeps in things like plankton (microscopic ocean animals) and hordes of jellyfish. All three reduce water clarity, and the jellyfish occasionally sting your crew for good measure.

Two: plankton distortion. Even assuming you have a tolerably clear and calm sea, plankton and sand are always in the water. And even if it's invisible to the human eye, it reflects the light in strange ways onto a camera lens, reducing visibility and contrast. Even more strange is what happens to color in the deep: it's enough to make you see red—if you could. At twenty-five feet below sea level, the colors of the spectrum begin to vanish. Red is the first to go, so anything red seen at, say, fifty feet—even blood—looks blue-green. In fact, the deeper you get, what you don't light, you probably won't see at all. Since you can't light up the whole ocean, you settle for key lighting and special filters and pray that the background sunlight filtering down will provide enough ambience illumination of colors, textures, and depths of field to create an effective image on screen.

Three: temperature. Working in warm, 80–degree water is equivalent to working in a bathing suit in 42–degree air, since water draws heat away from the human body very quickly. It may feel pleasant at first, but soon the body is struggling to maintain itself at 98.6 degrees. Wetsuits help by allowing a thin layer of water next to the skin which warms quickly and helps maintain body temperature. Al Giddings has designed good-looking wetsuits for the crew, but even so, the cold will eventually force us to limit their time in the water. And for our stars, who will not be wearing wetsuits in several underwater sequences for aesthetic reasons, the diving time will be cut to almost nil. Working time in the deep is predetermined, too, by the most basic physical law of diving: namely, you have to come up periodically for air. The physical effects of repeatedly going under and coming up are very tiring—in fact, between cold, changes in water pressure, ocean current, and simple physical exertion, diving is exhausting. And our divers will be fighting all the elements—plus juggling all the paraphernalia needed to make a feature motion picture—for eight hours every day.

Four ...

At least our hypothetical underwater cameras have materialized. Working around the clock for ninety days, Al Giddings has come through with three new cameras for tens of thousands of dollars in equipment, no charge for the priceless ingenuity or countless man-hours involved. Al has named his new creation the Petermar, in honor of all the "Peters" working on *The Deep*. Now, rarely do I see a piece of equipment that makes me want to wax lyrical over its beauty, but our new cameras are really gorgeous instruments, and Al has every right to feel like a proud papa. The Petermars are small and sleek, housed in shiny Ferrari-red watertight aluminum cases—the photographic counterparts of a sexy new Italian sports car. And they're just as beautiful inside. Al began with compact Arriflex cameras, outfitted them with Panavision lens systems, and then added such refinements as a "dome port"— a glass hemisphere over the lens—and other optical engineering to compensate for the visual distortions of filming in water. The cameras are electrically driven, capable of high-speed, slow motion, and standard shooting speeds, with complete flexibility of focus and aperture and a wide range of interchangeable lenses. All told, they weigh just seventy-five pounds on land, and in the water, all of eight ounces! Maybe, just maybe, our gamble has paid off.

The weather during our first few days on Peter Island has not been terrific and today, July 5, was no exception. We'd all entertained the stubborn hope that the clouds would magically dissipate and the wind obligingly die down for the first day of filming. No such luck. George Marler, the local dive shop owner who was renting us equipment and helping out on the shoot, invited some of us to meet the local weather man to see how things will shape up over the next few days.

Well, the Peter Island Weather Bureau turned out to be a one-room shack at the foot of the hill, and its resident forecaster, a scantily-clad black man chopping coconuts open on the wooden floor. He greeted us warmly, foisted some local brew into our hands, and listened to the questions George asked him. The weatherman obligingly delivered a forecast, but I couldn't understand a word of his strange vocabulary and exotic Caribbean accent. After we left, I had to pump George.

"So, what'd he say?"

"When the full moon comes, the water will be perfect for filming, calm and clear."

"When's the full moon?"

"In a few days."

"Oh." At least the unorthodox forecast satisfied George.

Meanwhile, the full moon is not yet upon us. On most locations, you can juggle the schedule around and get in some different types of filming if the weather isn't good. But we're in BVI to do underwater filming *only*. There are no surface or land shots—much less interior shots—that we can do to fill the time while waiting for sea conditions to improve; those are all going to be done later in Bermuda. We have to start filming *something,* so clouds or no clouds, we've begun this morning what will become our BVI routine.

Denny Breese, our divemaster (charged with the safety of crew and control of equipment) piloted us out at 7 A.M. on his boat, the *Tern,* to our wreck filming site. There, we hooked up with *Moby II,* an eighty-five-foot, fully equipped utility vessel captained by her roly-poly young owner, "Moby," which Al had commissioned out of Miami as our floating film studio. Once we'd all clambered aboard, the first "skull session" of the day began.

Skull sessions are lengthy briefings during which every aspect of the shots to be done below have to be worked out completely because communication in the deep, while possible, is severely limited. There are some basic signals available to divers like "come this way" and "out of air," which are fine for just paddling around snapping photographs of coral. But for the complex communication required on a feature film production, those signals, and even a few others like "action" and "cut," just don't make it.

So before each and every dive we will have sessions that are very much like two-minute football drills, reviewing two or three "plays" at once. This is where Yates' and Masters' storyboards will prove invaluable. Yates, Giddings, and Waterman discuss each segment of filming, then Yates briefs the entire cast and crew on the shots to be made. On a large blackboard lashed to one side of the deck, Al and Stan diagram exactly where every key of light and camera will be set up. All divers are listed so that everyone topside knows at a glance who's below. And only then does our underwater team go down to the remains of the *R.M.S. Rhone*.

The *Rhone*—our *Goliath*—is a 310-foot British steamer which sank in a hurricane with 125 men aboard on her maiden voyage in 1865. The eighty-year disparity between that date and World War II is actually no problem, because the *Rhone* is a metal-sided ship not much different in appearance from those Britain built decades later. The *Rhone* angles down from forty to ninety feet below the ocean's surface, and after 111 years it remains remarkably intact, much of its hull and rigging still in place. And like many wrecks, over the years it has become a kind of artificial reef, dripping with living rainbows of marine vegetation and large schools of even more fancifully colored fish. The *Rhone*'s bow section is home to a reclusive 175-pound jewfish who refuses to pose for photographs.

But the old boy has plenty of pursuers. The *Rhone* is a dazzling enough sight to be one of the most popular "dives" for underwater photographers in BVI. As such, it's a source of considerable income for Bert and Jacki Kilbride, old friends of Stan Waterman who live and run a local dive facility on BVI's Saba Rock, possibly the smallest inhabited island in the world at three-quarters of an acre! Well, we can't exactly post "keep out" signs around a Caribbean shipwreck, but we can't have stray scuba divers populating our mysterious *Goliath,* either. So we've asked Bert and Jacki to keep their diving tours away for six weeks. And we partially made it up to them by hiring tall, auburn-haired Jacki for *The Deep* as an underwater stunt double for Jacqueline Bisset.

Filling in for Nick Nolte during our first few days in BVI is another expert diver, Jack McKenney, who, with his well-built, blond good looks, is an excellent match for Nick. McKenney is a veteran diver and underwater photographer who put in eight years at *Skin Diver Magazine* before getting restless and returning to the deep. Also on the scene is Howard Curtis, a certified diver and veteran film stunt man who will double for Robert Shaw when necessary. Curtis, in fact, has doubled Shaw on his last two pictures, *Swashbuckler* and *Black Sunday,* and Shaw requested him for *The Deep.* The rest of the underwater team Al and Stan have gathered is comprised of professional divers and underwater filmmakers from all around the world. Even our continuity supervisor, Geri Murphy, is a diver first and a script girl second.

Al and Stan chose the third member of their Petermar team, Chuck Nicklin. Chuck's career is in many ways analogous to Al Giddings' in San Francisco, though further down the California coast: Chuck ran a dive shop and worked in underwater photography in San Diego. In fact, the two have been friendly competitors for fifteen years, and their relationship has taught all of us landlubbers a unique aspect of this new universe we had entered.

The world of diving, though it spans the globe, is actually a small scene in which everyone knows or at least knows of everyone else. For our underwater team, *The Deep* is like a family reunion. Probably never before has one film provided employment for so many, and all are doing splendidly.

But the most important part of our BVI shoot is yet to come: when our stars themselves will dive the *Rhone. The Deep* will be making film history . . . that is, if we can actually get our cast into the water.

We don't dare hope to see our stars dive for more than a few establishing shots while in BVI. Most of their diving work will be done in the controlled atmosphere of the Bermuda underwater set. However, Shaw and Nolte are both athletic, eager to learn, and have already picked up the rudiments of the sport without too much trouble during some preliminary lessons back in Los Angeles. They won't be ready to hop down to the *Rhone* immediately, but hopefully, after a few more lessons with George Marler and his assistant, Murray Maxwell, they'll be able to make a few dives during the thirty-five day shoot in the Caribbean. Shaw isn't due for another few days, but Nolte has already graduated from the Peter Island Yacht Club pool and is ready to try diving in the ocean.

July 8

Jacqueline Bisset is another story. This lovely, ethereal lady has many attributes, but an inclination toward sports and a love of water are not foremost among them. In fact, back when Jackie first signed on as Gail, she was so afraid of the water that she could hardly be lured into her own swimming pool. Rather than hire some local instructor, I brainstormed the idea of sending Al Giddings himself from San Francisco to L.A. to introduce Jackie to diving while she was still in home territory. I hoped it would be the start of a special relationship that would ease Jackie into diving once she arrived in BVI. And it has worked . . . sort of. Still, it will take a lot of time before Bisset feels at all comfortable with diving.

I for one can't blame her!

5

THE CAMERA SHUTTERS

Today was the big day for me—I received the helpful push from David Begelman described in our first chapter. I absolutely had to grit my teeth and try to learn how to dive, too. Throwing a lady into the drink without even getting my own toes wet didn't seem right somehow. So I reluctantly began my own diving lessons—and my own education in just what this whole crazy enterprise is *really* all about.

A scuba diving course is both physical and psychological, a blend of underwater physiology and consciousness-raising. Instructor Murray Maxwell explained the first principle of diving, simple but crucial: you must be totally calm and in touch with yourself at all times. The biggest danger of scuba diving lies not in malevolent marine life, but in human error and panic. And there is one cardinal rule; *never* panic and rush to the surface. That's how you get the notorious bends.

Murray likened a person's lungs to two balloons, filled to capacity with air each time he or she breathes. But at sixty feet undersea, the actual *amount* of air in a diver's lungs is nearly twice what it would be on the surface, because the pressure of the water compresses the air to half its normal volume for each thirty feet of depth. That means even if you think you're out of air at sixty feet below, you actually have more than you think you do in your lungs—probably enough to make it to the top if you just stay cool. If you don't, the effects can be treacherous.

The air compressed at sixty feet below expands in volume as you rise in the water, and it could literally burst your chest if you don't exhale it. Luckily, holding your breath in such circumstances takes incredible determination. A second, more real danger involves ascending too quickly. Oxygen combines chemically with the body; but nitrogen, another component of air, does not. Underwater, all that compressed nitrogen accumulates in the body tissues. When ascending, you have to do it slowly to give your body time to diffuse that extra nitrogen through your lungs, or else it will try to get rid of the rapidly expanding gas in the form of bubbles. Carbonation, a delight in your soda, is a disaster in your bloodstream, where it's capable of causing paralysis, agonizing pain, and death.

The rule of thumb is to rise no faster than your slowest exhaled bubbles, which is generally about the right speed to safely avert the bends. But if a diver goes under again and again in a limited time period, so much nitrogen builds up in his body that he finally has to "decompress" by hanging out underwater for anywhere from a few minutes to a few hours to give his body time to diffuse the excess gas.

That's why a divemaster is so crucial to the health and safety of "deepers." Denny Breese functions as a kind of dive security officer, keeping tabs on who's below, when they go down, and how long they spend at what depth. With this information and the aid of an intricate table especially designed for the purpose, Denny can compute how much decompression time is necessary. He then relays this information below over a hydrophone which broadcasts his voice via underwater speaker. Denny is well-qualified for the work. A boyish, cherubic-looking man, he's been diving since 1948 and has done everything from designing underwater habitats to salvaging nuclear weapons off the coast of Spain.

Anyway, I was still busy trying to remember how to clear my mask of water and equalize the air pressure in my ears. The pressure changes when you go down into the sea just as it does when you go up in a plane, but more painfully, because the depth creates *more* pressure on your ears, not less. The uneven pressure can be equalized with a few little tricks, among them a series of good, determined swallows, but it takes some concentration even to master these. So I had more than enough to keep me occupied, without thinking about the bends and the mindbending mathematical tables you have to consult to avoid them.

When Murray said I was ready to try diving in the ocean I was terrified. But Begelman's phone call was another terror, and so, at last, I confronted the mystique of the deep. Even with other divers nearby, there is a near-total silence underwater, broken only by the hollow, rhythmic sound of your own breathing that brings an almost mystical sense of solitude and peace. The weightlessness of your body in water is liberating. And the world beneath the sea is spectacular. I can only hope that our film will convey not only the terror of *The Deep* but its fantastic beauty as well, and that while scaring our audience to death, it will also turn some intrigued viewers on to the fascinations of the undersea world.

So my first experience in the ocean was, all told, positive enough to make me philosophical. Meanwhile, Nick Nolte was lucky to get out alive.

Nick almost swam headlong into catastrophe his first day in the sea. Murray Maxwell was about twenty feet ahead as he guided Nick down to a depth of 100 feet. Nick, breathing easily and calmly, suddenly took a breath of—nothing. No air. He pulled again. Nothing. He grabbed his gauge and looked at it—empty. By this time Murray was about twenty-five feet below him and still descending. Nick looked up. It was a free ascent in seventy feet of water, or a race of twenty-five feet down to Murray.

With long strokes he lunged down quickly and grabbed Murray's flipper. Murray swung around to see Nick slicing his index finger across his throat, trying to say, "I need air!" Immediately, Murray gave Nick his mouthpiece, and the two buddy-breathed, sharing the air from Murray's tank by passing the mouthpiece back and forth all the way to the surface.

Nick had kept his cool and his life, and had learned an important lesson: always check your own air tank and equipment before diving. Rely on no one. Nick's calm and ease in the water impressed both Murray Maxwell and George Marler, and they agreed that he can start diving the wreck to get the feel of it before he begins filming.

You would think that the least we could do for our diving film stars would be to provide nice weather for their exploits, but the weather continues to be lousy. In fact, Mother Nature has found a variety of ways to kick up her heels. Every time we turn around there's a whole new set of circumstances to deal with. Sunlight, wind, ocean surge, plankton, jellyfish invasions —all are changing daily, sometimes even from dive to dive. Peter Yates is a real trouper, carrying on with close-ups, which require less water clarity than longer shots, and a mischievous sense of humor. One evening, after a long and wearying day, Al Giddings and Jacki Kilbride had to decompress for over an hour below, so a team member was sent down with a *Playboy* centerfold to entertain them. Yates, up on *Moby II,* knew his gift had hit the mark when the casual intermittent air bubbles they had been sending up began spewing in a crazy foam on the ocean's surface. Thirty feet below, Giddings and Kilbride were laughing.

The grim weather is refining more than our senses of humor—it's also sharpening our skull sessions, which have been expanded to predict *precisely* what the crew will find when they actually get down to the *Rhone* each time. Can you imagine any film production being conducted in utter silence except for a few hand signals? No way!

Well, as the novices among us have discovered, divers have their own ingenious ways of verbally communicating underwater. One is to use Desco equipment, which features a full face mask connected by tubes to air tanks on the surface. The diver's mouth is free, so he can simply shout through his mask and be heard four or five feet away. But even without Desco, a determined diver can "talk" to his companions underwater. Chuck Nicklin and Al Giddings carry on whole conversations by "nose shouting" right through their mouthpieces—forming words in their throat without moving their lips. The result is muffled, kind of like talking through a gag, but understandable. And George Marler is an expert "glove speaker." George takes a breath of air from his mouthpiece, removes the glove from his hand, holds it up to his mouth, and speaks, producing a perfectly clear sentence before he replaces his mouthpiece.

We've just decided that these picturesque techniques will be as useful in front of the cameras as they are behind them. After all, beautiful underwater visuals and spooky sound effects notwithstanding, the spoken word conveys urgency and meaning as nothing else can. So we'll exploit the fact that David and Treece wear Desco in three "dives" by giving them some underwater dialogue, and "nose-shouting" and "glove-speaking" bits are being written in, too.

July 9

Our stars are the objects of a great deal of surreptitious attention. Surprisingly, our two romantic leads are both loners.

Nick Nolte was up and active early this morning. He played tennis and afterwards washed out his own clothes in the ocean. Nick is a very self-sufficient man, used to doing things for himself. He's a lot more complicated than the easy-going jock he first appears to be.

Bisset, we are learning, is an equally intriguing personality. She is sometimes very charming, loose, almost coltishly lively. But, like Nick, she tends to be rather reserved around people she doesn't know well—unfortunately, this category includes Nick. The two of them had a series of brief, inconclusive encounters in our early weeks in BVI, the "vibrations" between them civil, but ever-so-slightly testy. Admittedly, it isn't the most natural atmosphere in which to get to know someone, especially since the crew is watching their every move with goggle-eyed anticipation to see whether something suitably torrid is in the offing.

But there are professional reasons, too, for everybody's curiosity. The relationship between David and Gail has already undergone a quantum leap in intensity in the transition from book to shooting script. A new tension and ambiguity has been gained by changing them from newlyweds on honeymoon to passionate, troubled lovers on vacation together. Nolte and Bisset will be playing one sensual love scene during which, with any luck at all, sparks will fly on screen. So we're watching carefully to see what sort of electricity is generated in their off-screen encounters. Each wants to get to know the other, but neither seems to quite know how to go about it. You can't exactly play matchmaker in a situation like this. Whatever is going to happen between these two will just have to happen naturally.

For days now, we've been shooting without ever seeing one frame of anything we've done. We've been biting our nails in suspense, right through our diving gloves. In Hollywood, you trot your exposed film over to the lab on Tuesday night and it's back for viewing Wednesday afternoon. That evening, you can watch what you did just the day before, and make any adjustments necessary—new shots, angles, lighting, whatever.

Way out on foreign location, when you're spending money like sea water, it's even more crucial that you see your exposed footage as soon as possible. But for all we knew, we could have been filming since we got to BVI with a jammed camera shutter, since it would be five days and about $175,000 later that we'd find out.

Our film has to make the trip toward the New York lab back through Tortola, Beef Island, and San Juan. Once our film cans reach Kennedy Airport, U.S. customs agents have to open them up in special darkrooms to make sure they contain nothing but film. If the film arrives past a certain time, the procedure has to be postponed until the next day. Only then would our film get developed and printed—and checked again at the airport before wending its long way back to us.

July 10

Finally—finally!—we saw rushes today from the first few days of shooting. Instant trauma. We had depended largely on natural light and had lit the *Rhone* as sparingly as possible for a realistic effect. But even with colorful backgrounds and an occasional sun-dappled coral, the overall mood of the footage was oppressively dark and gloomy—OK for a Czech art film, maybe, but not too desirable for an exciting adventure movie. Besides, *The Deep* is definitely a summer picture. That means large drive-in audiences . . . and dark film images are all but invisible on drive-in screens.

As you can well imagine, this left us feeling pretty glum, and we were counting on at least our night dailies to hit the mark. So the projector was rethreaded, the lights turned off, and we all settled back eagerly again in the darkness.

Twenty seconds passed. The screen remained pitch black. We could hear film whirring through the camera, all right, but we couldn't see a damn thing. A few nervous questions shot around the room. "Uh . . . is the projector light on?" "Is there film in the machine?"

We sat there in complete darkness for about four minutes. Finally, one small pinpoint of light traveled slowly across screen like a lit cigarette arcing through a pitch-black room. At that, cheers and laughs could be heard.

It was black humor in more ways than one, but it wasn't really very funny. If the day rushes were disappointing, the night dailies were utter disaster, and every one of us knew it. Chris Challis, our spry and sprightly British Director of Photography, came to the rescue. Non-diving Chris has no work to do on *The Deep* until the company goes on to Bermuda, and actually just dropped into BVI to see how things are going. "Let's shoot the scene day for night," he suggested.

"Day for what?" Waterman and Giddings and Nicklin asked.

Day for night is a filming technique that simply involves placing a special filter over the camera lens, or in our case—since we had no such filter at hand—filming by day with the camera aperture stopped down. This retains enough natural light to see by, while creating the darker, more mysterious look of evening. It's an old Hollywood trick, but not surprisingly, Giddings, Waterman, and Nicklin are just a wee bit skeptical. It has certainly never been done before underwater.

Yates, too, has his doubts. While he is well acquainted with day for night, Yates is known in the film industry as something of a stickler for authenticity. As one wag has remarked, "Peter would never allow a Cadillac purring on the soundtrack if the hero is seen driving a Mercedes Benz." But happily, Yates blends that scrupulous sense of filmic reality with an awareness of the realities of filmmaking. He talked over the day for night with Giddings and Waterman, and they've agreed to try it. If nothing else, it can only improve what we just saw up there on screen.

"We'll get it," he assured me calmly. God, I hope so. At least the moon was full tonight. According to our native weatherman, the gradually improving skies and seas should be clearer and calmer thàn ever.

Back in Los Angeles, though, another sort of storm has been brewing. Columbia Pictures is starting to get mighty curious about just what we're doing out here in the Caribbean boonies at $35,000 a day. Somehow I don't think they'll take too kindly to a true report. "Well, we're getting lousy footage, see, but it's because the weather's bad, and this native weatherman who chops coconuts on the side says when the moon is full it'll all be terrific . . ." I have to send them something, if not deliver an all-out Show and Tell. Luckily, Stan Jaffe, my replacement at Columbia, has produced films himself and is sympathetic to our plight. So we've compromised on a plan to duplicate and send Columbia only selected materials. It's a tactic that has several advantages, not the least being that we can pick carefully and send Columbia only the scant cream of our mostly disappointing crop.

In spite of our success in temporarily keeping Big Daddy at bay, the gloom of the first week's dailies has spread inexorably to the mood of the crew. A snorkeling trip with Nick Nolte and my wife, Lynda, to the far side of the island was a respite from the growing tensions of the shoot, but even this idyllic afternoon ended on a harrowing (if humorous) note. Feeling pleasantly mellow as we walked along the shore, we didn't see a giant, fierce-looking 250–pound black pig standing up to its haunches in the water until we literally tripped on it! Its angry grunting and snorting discouraged Nick from retrieving half a pair of beloved, tattered old sneakers he'd left behind as he darted away, though he tried at first. The creature glared, grunted again, and began to wade ashore—and Lynda and I and a semi-barefoot Nick raced the hell out of there.

Back at the production office, more grunting and snorting was heard, this time from several crew members who've suddenly decided they want to renegotiate their deals. George Justin wasn't buying it though. He put his proverbial foot down and the grumblings gradually ceased.

Part of the reason for the hubbub, I think, is a confusion of professional roles that makes our team feel that all's fair in love and underwater fees. Derek Cracknell, our First Assistant Director, has lost some of the unquestioned authority of that position to *The Deep*. Much of our underwater team's loyalty is understandably with Al Giddings (in fact, they've adopted the nickname, "Giddings' Gorillas") and with Denny Breese who, as divemaster, is charged with the safety of the team. The crew of the *Moby II* listens to Moby, the ship's captain; while Peter Yates, our director, is considered the creative captain. Derek, Al, Stan, Denny, Moby—all need authority to do their jobs correctly. Not to mention my own problems as a neophyte producer *and* a neophyte diver, running around trying to keep tabs on it all. It hasn't resulted in overt differences, but the overlap gets confusing, and it must seem like a free-for-all to the crew at times.

But the real reason for the team's restiveness has little to do with work. It's mostly a case of good old island fever. The isolation which first seemed so romantic is rapidly wearing thin. There's really nothing to do except play tennis and scuba dive, and after working in the ocean for over eight hours a day, no crew member wants any more contact with water than that afforded by a nice hot shower. The food, while good, is taking on a paralyzing sameness, due in part to the fact that almost everything on the Club's menu is served with great globs of bernaise sauce on it And there's virtually no contact with the outside world. Radio broadcasts are near impossible to pick up and are usually in Spanish anyway. There's no television, and newspapers straggle in days after their printed date. We learned of the dramatic Israeli raid at Entebbe four days after it happened, and the Montreal Olympics during which Nadia Comaneci captivated much of the planet passed us by with hardly a flicker.

So, for lack of any other contact, we've turned to each other for companionship. Most crew members spend their evenings together in the Yacht Club bar, but it's getting awfully boring around here. We've been so restless that tonight, when underwater photographer Dave Doubilet, who just arrived on Peter Island, brought his banjo out after dinner, we all crowded around him as if he were the first wireless set. Back home, we'd hardly have blinked an eye. But after a steady diet of steelband and calypso, Dave fingerpicking his banjo sounded as good to us as an angel plucking a heavenly harp.

Still, many of the crew are beginning to lust after more than just wine and song. Being on Peter Island is an exercise in frustration that the camaraderie of the team does nothing to relieve.

The growing tension exploded into a full-throttle confrontation in the dining room when Nick announced to Yates that he felt ready to begin filming on the *Rhone*.

"I'll tell you when you're ready to begin filming," Yates replied curtly.

"I know I'm ready!" Nick persisted.

"Look," Al Giddings said sternly, "you're not ready to go down to begin filming on the *Rhone* until you've dived it first."

"But I've been diving the *Rhone* for two days already!" Nick shrilled, which happened to be true.

Al hadn't known a thing about it!

July 11

So Nick was aboard *Moby II* when it pulled out from its moorings yesterday morning. As the crew prepared for the first diving sequence, Divemaster Denny Breese heard a weak distress call over *Moby II*'s radio. A forty-foot cruiser, *Pieces of Eight,* was sinking in heavy seas with three men aboard. Al, Stan, Denny, and two other crew members managed to get a fix on the craft and raced over on the *Tern*. The boat was literally sinking as Al and Stan plunged into the ocean and rescued its occupants: two elderly men, one with an artificial hip, and a younger man who couldn't swim. Seconds after the three men were hauled aboard the *Tern*, *Pieces of Eight* tipped and sank like a stone in 150 feet of water.

After that *Sea Hunt*-style adventure, the rest of the day was pleasantly anticlimactic. The water was clearer than it has been for days, Nick performed like a charm, and some key shots were taken of him at the wreck. Nick was so pleased with the day's work that he promptly wandered off and drank too much last night, paying his dues for it this morning with a fierce hangover. Unlike our underwater team—who seem to have wooden legs, drinking all night (against every rule in any diving manual) but showing up religiously at 7 A.M. every morning—he apparently hasn't yet learned the fine art of mixing booze and sea water. But Nick's total ease in the water has convinced us that he can be used in most of his own underwater filming from now on, something we never counted on or even expected.

Jacqueline Bisset, though, is still skittish about diving. Jacki Kilbride is a terrific double, but the film's impact hinges on getting Bisset herself to do some key scenes in the ocean. But Jackie B. is still terrified to go below twenty feet in the ocean, though the wreck at its shallowest end is forty-five feet deep and we're filming mostly at sixty to eighty feet under. Her body movements in the water are as stiff as a marionette's, and an anxious scowl is clearly visible even through her mask. Jackie is especially spooked by the occasional jellyfish invasions we experience around the *Rhone* . . . thousands of the creatures wafting in with the tide, glowing eerily in the light, and yes, stinging the crew fiercely. They're certainly unpleasant to encounter, and they account in large part for Jackie's wariness. It's just as well that she doesn't know there are barracuda down there, too.

One evening, after a particularly long day, Al Giddings and George Marler had made so many dives that they were still decompressing thirty feet below long after the rest of the crew had returned to the surface. As they hung there, George suddenly spotted an ominous sight: two six-foot-plus barracudas, sharp teeth flashing and beady eyes gleaming, slowly coming right at them.

George tapped Al on the shoulder, and the two men eased close together and remained motionless. The two giant fish came up to them and then, as if in some underwater ballet, separated and went right around them. The barracudas turned around and gazed back at Al and George as if to think it over; then, apparently deciding that this strange, gangly two-headed creature could prove more trouble than it was worth, they moved off into the dark waters.

At a small barbeque at Guber Gulch tonight, Al recounted the incident casually to a wide-eyed audience. "After all," Al concluded, "barracuda really aren't as ferocious as they're cracked up to be."

Fascinated, I quietly asked Stan, who knows Al well, if, in all of Al's diving experiences, he'd ever been really frightened by anything he encountered.

Stan Waterman is unequalled in his ability to tell a story, and when he's not busy filming underwater he's making the lecture circuit, hypnotizing spellbound audiences with true-life tales of the deep. He had us in the palm of his hand as he told the following one.

In the late 1950's, Al ran a dive shop in Northern California with a friend named Leroy, who was both best buddy and business partner to Al. The two sold diving equipment and led diving tours in the San Francisco area.

One day, Al and Leroy took a boat with about twenty-five divers to some reefs off the Farallon Islands, about twenty-five miles north of San Francisco. The day's dive was over. Most of the divers were back on board, and Al and Leroy were only about thirty yards from the boat. Suddenly Al heard an ungodly scream, several octaves higher than anything he knew the human voice was capable of producing. At first he thought it might have been one of the girls in the group fooling around on the ship.

But as Al turned around, he saw the the scream had come from Leroy, less than ten yards away from him in the water. Leroy's face was white with horror. "Oh, my God, my legs!" he screamed. Al now saw the water ripple behind Leroy's head as the fin of a great white shark poised to attack glided in. Then Leroy was yanked straight down, disappearing into the sea with another chilling scream.

The sea filled with blood and Al, still with his diving equipment on his back, began to swim toward Leroy. By this time everyone in the group had seen the shark and those still in the water had frantically clambered up the ladder and anchor chains to the boat. All now watched in horror as Al approached the spot where Leroy had gone under.

Suddenly Leroy came catapulting to the surface again, screaming at the top of his lungs. Al knew he was risking his own life to try and save his friend's. But he shot his hand out to Leroy and began to pull him toward the ship. At any moment, Al knew the shark would strike again. Leroy twisted and turned and screamed in the water, trying to climb up over Al.

Finally, Al was able to get Leroy hauled up onto the deck as his friend's blood rained down on him. Now Al was alone in the ocean, his own legs dangling appetizingly in the blood-filled waters.

With all his strength, Al hauled himself out of the water, with his heavy equipment still on his back. He looked down at Leroy and realized what a monstrous creature they both had just escaped. In one stroke, the shark had removed his friend's full right calf and the full right cheek of his buttock. Leroy's exposed arteries pulsed like telephone wires strung out on the deck, and he was losing blood in enormous quantities. But Al had saved Leroy's life, and ultimately his leg was saved, too. Al just collapsed, stunned at what he'd been through—not in some exotic South Pacific location, but right in his own backyard.

When the story was over, Al sat and gazed into space, living the horror of it again for what must have been the hundredth time. The rest of us were quiet, too. We had just learned more about Al Giddings than anything in his impressive ten-page resumé, or days of work under less frightening circumstances, could have told us.

6

RAPTURE OF THE DEEP

~~~~~~

July 11

Robert Shaw is in the British Virgin Islands. And he is not very happy.

Shaw arrived at BVI airport with an incredible entourage: his nine children, secretary-companion Virginia Jansen, a housekeeper, and sixty-five pieces of luggage. There's scarcely room on all of Peter Island for a household of this size, let alone the Yacht Club. So a house for Shaw & Co. has been rented on Tortola, from which he can take the ferry either over to Peter Island or directly to the wreck site each morning.

But first, he wanted to tell us his reaction to the script we'd given him, and he wasted no time in getting right down to brass tacks. He immediately launched into a detailed analysis of the screenplay's flaws and weaknesses—rather accurately, it was later admitted. Tom Mankiewicz was hired for just this reason. "Well, Robert," said Yates, "we have writer Tom Mankiewicz here, and the script is still in the work, so why don't we sit down and thrash out some ideas together?" Which is just what they did.

Shaw has also set about brushing up on his diving, and now an entirely different problem looms. It's not how to get Shaw *into* the ocean that worries us any more . . . it's how to keep him *out!* Shaw, accompanied by his children parading around in their own pint-sized tanks, has taken a few more lessons, has mastered the sport, and is already restless to begin filming on the *Rhone*. Robert Shaw can be a quirky fellow. Rather than confront us directly, he called his agent, John Gaines, in Hollywood, who in turn called me on Peter Island to ask why we haven't started using Robert yet! We asked him—and Robert—to just be patient, and Shaw has finally settled for going out on *Moby II* and diving down to watch the shoot until his own scenes are scheduled.

The script situation, too, has been resolved happily. Shaw and Mankiewicz hit it off right away, and work very smoothly together. The two of them came up almost immediately with a number of subtle changes in character and dialogue that make significant change for the better. Shaw was unselfish with his contribution of time, energy and, most of all, talent. Now the fiery actor is equally passionate about his pleasure with the film, and over dinner tonight, he ecstatically insisted on betting his percentage of profits against mine that *The Deep* would be one of the top-ten grossing films of the last ten years. Knowing that my percentage was larger, I naturally refused. So Shaw suggested we bet a dinner. "OK," I agreed. "Dinner for two," he continued, "anywhere in the world, every year for the rest of our lives!" So that's the bet I have with Robert Shaw, and even with those stakes, I'm still praying I lose.

Getting Robert Shaw to feel high about the film was a major coup. And then, today, another break: Jacqueline Bisset finally dove the *Rhone!*

Not without some more agonizing, though. After days and days, Al Giddings realized that much of Jackie's trouble stemmed from the fact that a crucial piece of diving equipment, the regulator, was not supplying her air at a comfortable rate. So, just change it, you say? Well, it wasn't that simple because we'd already shot a fair amount of footage with Jackie Kilbride using an identical regulator, and with a new one, the film wouldn't match up. But it was a choice between giving Bisset a new regulator or *never* getting her down to the *Rhone*. Then luck struck—a new regulator of the same style arrived in the daily mail and Jackie gave it a try.

The change was dramatic. Jackie was suddenly much more relaxed in the water, and dove to sixty feet with no trouble!

The best surprise of all, though, came tonight when we viewed some dailies featuring Bisset underwater. Stan Waterman said it all: "She's the only woman I ever saw who looks beautiful even in a face mask!" Further south she was a treat, too, a vision in brief bikini bottom and clinging white T-shirt. All of us were ecstatic about this lovely and sensual sight, and the most excited of all was Jackie herself. She now insists on doing all her own shots on the *Rhone* to make sure that everyone knows it's really her down there—even to the point of redoing what's already been done by her double. Quite a turnaround for someone who couldn't be begged or bribed into the ocean just days ago.

July 14

Jackie isn't the only spectacular sight onscreen these days. After the initial miseries of watching early rushes, daily viewing is suddenly a positive treat. Our day for night filming turned out just as we wanted: richly mysterious, but with the pertinent action nicely highlighted. Chris Challis has even learned how to dive so he can go down to the *Rhone* every day to personally supervise the lighting set-up. We've also learned that our original dailies weren't bad after all. For some reason, the lab had been printing them too dark and too green, but the negatives yielded the brighter, more colorful footage we sought when reprinted correctly. And Al's cameras are performing splendidly. In fact, if it weren't for the bubbles our actors exhaled, it would be easy to forget that they're even underwater! So things are looking up for *The Deep*, and just in time, too: our first press visitors are about to descend on us.

An unbelievable day!

Film publicity is always a tricky business. Many journalists, even as they're being wined and dined, have a depressingly good nose for bad news. Naturally, we wanted to counteract any muckraking impulses by putting our best flipper forward. But there we were on a work boat which, while it served our filming purposes well, would get a bit cramped with hordes of reporters tromping around on deck. And our publicity trump card—the fact that our stars were now actually doing their own ocean diving—is happening eighty feet under. How were we going to get reporters enthusiastic about something they couldn't even see? Well, the answer was obvious. In addition to the standard fare, lunch with the cast and all that, we decided to include an optional diving lesson in our press itinerary.

Far-fetched? Maybe. Certainly not every reporter would follow the trail of a story down to a century-old shipwreck in the Caribbean. But our first press visitors, writer Nancy Collins and photographer Peter Simins, of the trendy, gossipy *Women's Wear Daily*, were spunky souls. And after one scuba lesson in the pool, they were escorted down to the *Rhone*, where they were amply rewarded for their nerve.

No sooner had Nancy and Peter descended than the water shifted and suddenly, for the first time since we've begun filming, there was magnificent 100-foot visibility in every direction! Yates and Giddings ecstatically began to shoot those long, rich establishing shots of Nick and Jackie on the wreck that we'd all waited so long for. *Thus Spake Zarathustra* began to boom out over the underwater loudspeaker, enhancing the mood of triumph. Assistant Director Derek Cracknell first brainstormed the idea of broadcasting taped classical music to entertain decompressing divers, and now we're playing the music to film by, as well. Diving D.J. Derek also provided some Strauss waltzes and Beethoven's Fifth for our listening pleasure today.

The *WWD* reporters were bowled over by the whole spectacle. Here was Jacqueline Bisset acting her heart out for three floating cinematographers with gorgeous bright red cameras trained on her, while script continuity girl Geri Murphy sat placidly on the ocean floor, taking notes on a special slate. Peter Yates made a great sight for the reporters as he came up between takes: a portly, aristocratic Englishman with bright robin's-egg-blue eyes, decked out in blue jeans and full diving regalia, rising radiantly out of the sea on his diving platform like Botticelli's Venus on her half-shell. "I've seen hush-hush Hollywood productions before," Nancy said in an awed voice back at the Yacht Club later. "But that was really a closed set!" Both she and Peter were totally won over to *The Deep,* and they assured us that we'll receive the first of what we hope will be many complimentary write-ups for our trouble.

More press is slated to arrive in their wake. We've tried to stagger our intricate publicity schedule, but it looks like the various press contingents will be stacking up on Peter Island like DC–10's over O'Hare Airport. Publicity coordination has become a juggling act, and I sort of feel less like a film producer than an overworked tour guide on the Disneyland Jungle Cruise.

Another delicate P.R. operation involves the government of the British Virgin Islands. *The Deep* is the first film ever to be shot in BVI, and both Hollywood and Roadtown want to keep things friendly. We walk on protocol pins and needles because when you're filming in a foreign country, what the local government giveth it can also taketh away as it sees fit. So we've tried like mad to make a good impression, but there have been a couple of gaffes. One night, Governor Wallace invited the entire company to a reception at his home. Eager to please, we turned up in suits, ties, the whole bit. The Governor and his family greeted us in casual summery outfits and expressions of puzzlement at our stiff formality. But diplomatic relations survived our faux pas and continue to be cordial.

We fare equally well with the local populace. All of us are aware that many Caribbean islands are hotbeds of social and racial unrest, and we're delighted to discover that BVI doesn't fit that mold. For the most part, its people are relaxed and easygoing. Except, that is, for the chaps Nick Nolte encountered one recent night.

That evening, Nick went into Tortola and dug up a native drinking partner, as he'd done before. Neither Nick nor his companions could ever understand a word the other said, but that was OK—"This round's on me" can quickly be communicated with a few deft waves of the hand.

According to Nick, he and this fellow were having a few rounds together, until everybody else left and the bartender wanted to go home. The Tortolan expansively invited Nick to continue the drinking session at his home, and Nick, after deciphering the message, nodded "sure."

They went to the guy's house and continued their revelry. Two other local guys and a woman wandered in. They were unfortunately the sort of locals who don't like big blond blue-eyed types around their women.

Well, Nick tried to explain that he's really not interested in the lady. He came up with some graphic gestures to say that he values affection (patting the left side of his chest) more than just getting laid (you can figure that one out). But the natives either weren't getting it or weren't buying it. They *were* starting to look convincingly threatening and began pushing Nick around. Luckily, Nick wasn't too far gone to deduce that all the clever charades in the world weren't going to get these guys off his back—which is just about where they were at this point. So without pausing for good-byes, Nick ducked out and bolted homeward, narrowly escaping them at the dock.

Except for that little incident, though, our relationship with the locals is, though limited, for the most part friendly. Our situation, in fact, is a perfect switch on the old joke: the natives are fine . . . it's the *visitors* who are restless! Our local contact, Anselmo, knows everyone and every place to go. With singsong accent, silver rings on all ten fingers and a little silver bauble in his ear, Anselmo comes off like the exotic heavy in a James Bond film. But underneath the glitter was a crackerjack "go-fer" to warm the heart of any Hollywood producer. Anselmo zipped back and forth between Tortola and Peter Island for all the little odds and ends we needed, saving *The Deep* on countless occasions from the disaster that looms on any production when you suddenly run out of something.

MAKING
THE DEEP

The Principals:
Treece (Robert Shaw),
David (Nick Nolte)
and Gail
(Jacqueline Bisset)
examine a Spanish
medallion—
the key to the
treasure buried in
The Deep.

The Peter Principle: author Peter Benchley, director Peter Yates, producer Peter Guber.

Yates confers with the
experts Al Giddings and Stan Waterman.
Notice the blackboard on which the underwater
cast and crew moves are plotted out.

Guber and Teddy Tucker, the real-life inspiration
for Romer Treece, on the wreck of the
Constellation, the real-life inspiration for the *Goliath.*

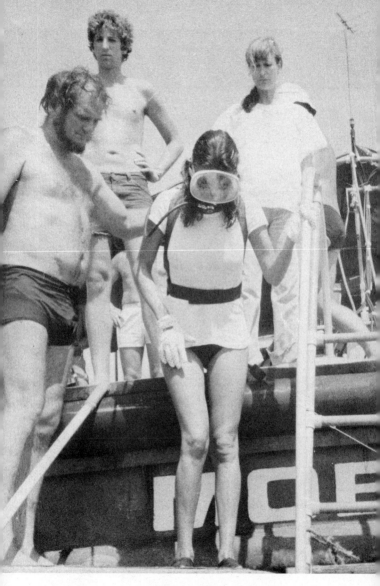

After a difficult first dive, Jacqueline Bisset,

ot giving up, goes at it again.

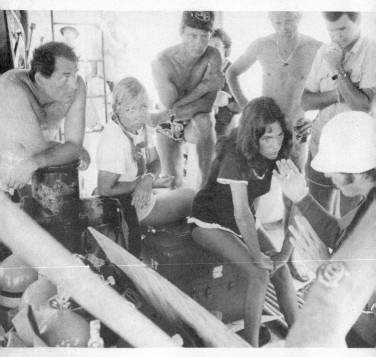

A "skull session"
aboard the *Moby II*.
Shaw and Bisset listen
intently as Giddings
explains a shot.

Al Giddings and one of the
Petermar cameras he designed and
built for *The Deep*.

Bisset, Shaw and Nolte set up the dredge
to escape marauding sharks for a key *Deep* sequence
filmed in the British Virgin Islands.

Robert Shaw (Treece) cuts the air hoses
so that he, Nick Nolte (David) and Jacqueline Bisset (Gail)
can ride up through the bubbles that will be created
in order to avoid the hungry sharks above.

Howard Curtis, doubling Robert Shaw, fends off sharks
Reef of Australia. On the next pages,
whirring even when a

during filming in the Coral Sea off the Great Barrier
Giddings's Gorillas keep their cameras
shark gets too close.

The B.U.S. as it appeared before one million gallons
dish-shaped urethane-lined excavation

of sea water was pumped in. In the center of the huge
rests a portion of the shipwreck set.

Yates directs a scene in the B.U.S.
Inside his face mask a
microphone relays his commands to
the surface which the divemaster then
broadcasts back down to the crew.

Bisset as Gail swims over a skeletal section of the *Rhone*.

Bisset and Nolte explore the *Rhone* and each other.

The hand-made treasure eventually
discovered beneath the wreck of the *Goliath*.

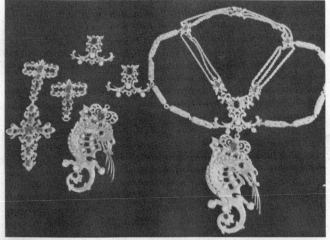

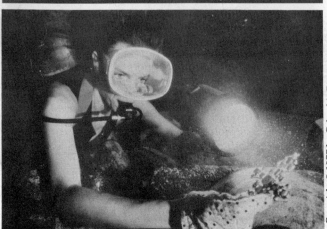

Jackie Bisset discovers the ruby-encrusted
cross in the grave of the *Grifon*.

Robert Shaw as Treece examines the
ampule discovered on the *Goliath* and realizes he's
stumbled on a long-lost cache of morphine.

Sketch by Tony Masters, the production

designer, of the interior of the *Rhone*.

Shaw and Nolte as Treece and David wend their way

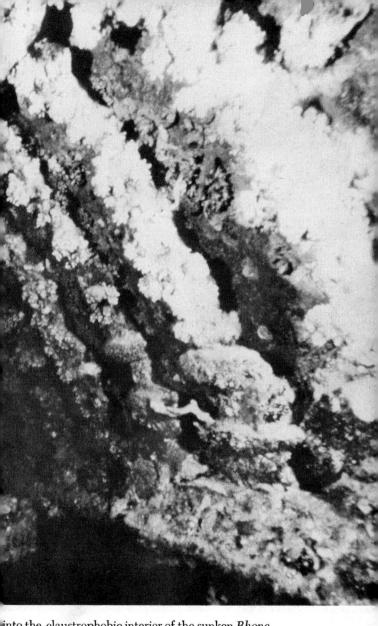

into the claustrophobic interior of the sunken *Rhone*.

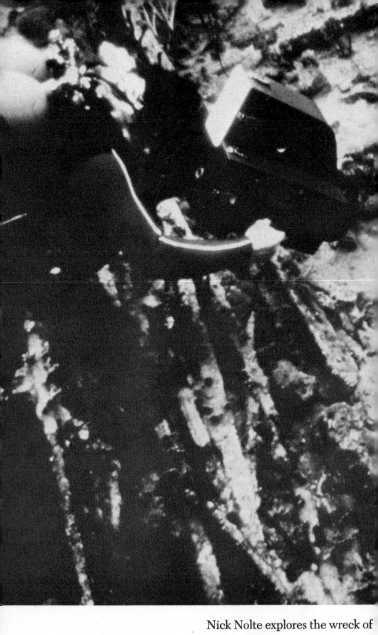

Nick Nolte explores the wreck of

the *Rhone* for Al Giddings's camera.

Jackie Bisset brings a
key image of *The Deep* to life:
Gail struggling alone
toward the surface from
the ocean's terrifying depths.

Bisset bolts from the deep in blind panic,
her face mask filling with blood.

The climactic fight between Treece and Cloche,
The lurking 12-foot eel

as conceived and sketched by Tony Masters.
is depicted in mid-strike.

Construction of the moray eel, nicknamed Percy. Walter Stones is seated on the dolly from which Percy's movements were controlled during filming. A production staffer examines the eel's fiberglass skull.

Charlie Spurgeon, co-creator of the 12-foot mechanical eel, touches up Percy's fearsome teeth.

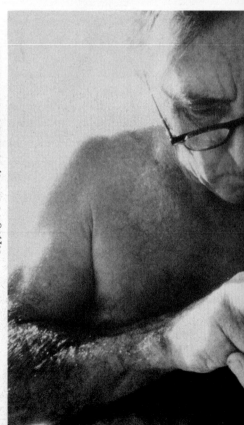

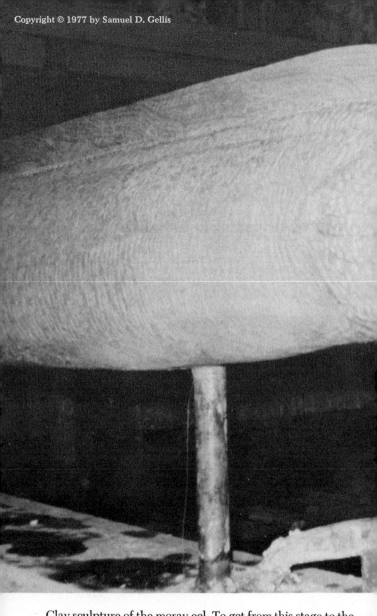

Clay sculpture of the moray eel. To get from this stage to the

final torso required a series of molds in plaster and fiberglass.

The special "squish" head of Lou Gossett is
placed in the eel's mouth to test lighting exposure.

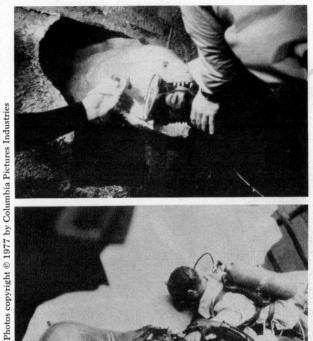

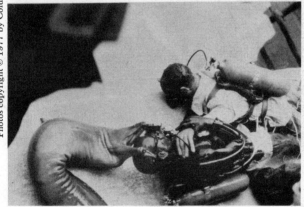

The half-size replicas of Shaw and Gossett are prepared
for filming with the live sedated eel.

The giant moray—real or mechanical?

Lou Gossett plays arch villain Henri Cloche. His "squish"

dummy head later becomes dinner for the moray eel.

The Orange Grove elevator as it was
conceived by Tony Masters for the major
fight sequence of the film.

The camera basket, hanging from a
135-foot crane, lowers Peter Yates and the shooting
team into position for the elevator sequence.

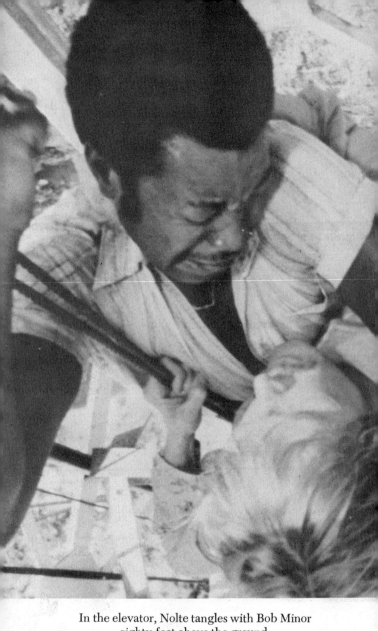

In the elevator, Nolte tangles with Bob Minor
eighty feet above the ground.

The carefully engineered explosion of Treece's lighthouse.

An intimate moment between Nolte and Bisset
as David Sanders and Gail Berke.

By now *The Deep* is falling prey to an ailment that nothing in the world can cure. Island Fever is epidemic; the near-total isolation of Peter Island is beginning to affect even the most stalwart souls. It's getting to be like *Gilligan's Island* without the punchlines. Our restless Gorillas are inventing ever more creative ways to release their excess energy. One night Al Giddings broke into Stan Waterman's room and, as Stan lay serenely asleep, unceremoniously dumped him out of dreamland and onto the floor. Still not satisfied, Al proceeded to dump Stan's mattress out of the second-floor window! What would have been breaking and entering back home was just a particularly amusing bit of gossip the next morning, and even Stan somehow got into the spirit of it all.

Mooning is another way to get rid of excess energy for many, including Nick, who once mooned the camera sixty feet below to indicate that a shot was day for night (the reaction of the Columbia brass to this particular slating procedure is unrecorded). Most moons, though, have no such professional excuse. On their way back from filming one evening, our ever-more-punchy crew began to moon passing boats. The moon also rose over a wild drunken party held at Guber Gulch. We got good and ripped on piña coladas and danced to ear-splitting music in various stages of undress. After we had finally retired, a new mattress-tossing contingent worked its way through our various cottages.

Despite such antics, though, the rigors and tensions of our shoot are getting us down. During many weeks, we work seven days straight, a schedule that's exhausting even on land; underwater, it's truly punishing. Just about the only good thing about all that diving is the fact that it burns up so many calories. "At least you don't have to worry about what you eat on this shoot!" exulted Peter Yates. "I think I'll open a skin-diving fat farm when this is all over." So we're fashionably svelte, all right, but we're also bleary-eyed from all the salt water and all the booze we drink to forget about it; sniffling, snuffling, fighting off infections and sheer bone-weariness every day.

It's not only the physical exertion and isolation that are such a bitch in BVI, either. Actors who are used to working on dialogue and character are floundering around in the ocean for weeks on end with hardly more than a nose-shout to deliver. Everyone is well aware of the danger that they'll be utterly exhausted, with their characters still as stiff as a new pair of shoes, by the time we begin filming in Bermuda. But had we started out daisy fresh and completed our land filming first, we'd have ended up on Peter Island smack at the height of the hurricane season. We're trapped either way, and there's nothing to do but cope or complain, or a fair amount of both.

About the only member of the company who isn't succumbing to island fever is Lou Gossett—partly because he arrived on Peter Island relatively late in the game, and partly because he's so relaxed it's hard to imagine him getting feverish at all. In fact, Lou Gossett is one of the nicest, most down-to-earth guys I've ever known, and it will take some real acting for him to play Cloche, our cunning villain. But Lou is up for the challenge—he's actually looking forward to playing a "classic villain"—and he immediately began diving lessons for the climactic scene when Cloche and his sidekick Ronald dive down to the wreck and engage in underwater battle with Treece and David. Lou's credentials as a diver are perfect, and with his graceful, rangy physique and calm personality he's picked up the sport easily.

Back at sea, the weather is up to its old tricks; not quite as bad as before, but after that one gorgeous afternoon, visibility is again only so-so. We've decided to go inside the wreck to begin work on the third dive, the dive that ends in *The Deep*'s big shark sequence.

What must be set up in this scene is the fact that both David and Treece are using Desco breathing gear as they work with the heavy piece of equipment known as the dredge, siphoning up huge amounts of sand from the grave of the Spanish galleon *Grifon*. Desco equipment has several advantages over standard diving gear. It frees your back from the weight of a tank and allows you to move about with freedom, stay below longer, and speak through the mask. But it also puts a good deal of distance between you and your air supply on the surface, which isn't so hot. For that reason Gail rejects Desco in favor of a conventional tank, and it turns out to be a life-saving decision for all three.

So as we began work on the early part of this scene today, we needed three film stars eighty feet down in the ocean and forty feet inside this huge shipwreck, two of them breathing on Desco gear and using heavy dredge equipment. There were 11,000 watts' worth of lighting bearing down through the water inside the *Rhone;* hoses, lines and wires tangled everywhere like so much spaghetti; and safety divers stationed in the corridor leading into the wreck's hull before our stars were ushered inside. Better than twenty-five people were now inside the wreck. Cameras, lights, and props strewn throughout turned the *Rhone*'s labyrinthine chambers into an underwater obstacle course.

Denny Breese was cringing on board, imagining everything that could go wrong below, and sure enough, something did—with the Desco, no less. Filming had barely begun when suddenly Denny's voice boomed out over the underwater loudspeaker. "THE DESCO HAS BROKEN DOWN! SURFACE IMMEDIATELY. DO NOT DECOMPRESS."

Nick and Robert dropped everything and began racing furiously out of the wreck, but they had to travel dozens of feet horizontally before they could even begin to surface! Safety divers were grabbing their hoses and reeling them in like fish to speed their journey. Finally Shaw and Nolte reached the opening and shot up together, hitting the surface safe, but more than a little shaken.

July 16

You don't throw orders like "SURFACE IMMEDIATELY" around in the deep, so Denny's dramatic announcement needs a bit of explanation here. Denny, manning the faulty equipment on *Moby II*, had quickly calculated that there was still enough air in the Desco tubes to get Shaw and Nolte to the surface, and since they'd just gone down, there was no need to decompress. If push had really come to shove, the actors could have buddy-breathed to the surface with crew members, though it would have meant ripping off their face masks to do so. Each member of our team was wearing a double air tank, which automatically comes equipped with an "octopus"—an extra regulator and mouthpiece hook-up. But there's no doubt that this crisis takes the prize as the most dangerous, claustrophobic, and complicated of our entire BVI shoot so far. The Desco was fixed, we resumed work on the scene with extra care, and at last we got the key shots we were going for. Only then did Denny Breese stop cringing.

The days are going quickly now, and we're pushing on to get the shots we need. Among the most crucial are those establishing Cloche and Ronald swimming down to the wreck as they go after David and Treece at the film's end. The actor we cast back in L.A. as Ronald—Earl Maynard—was not originally scheduled for the BVI trip since we'd told Earl that he wouldn't have to do his own underwater scenes. For some reason, it hadn't dawned on us that finding a stunt double for Earl would be about as easy as finding one for the Jolly Green Giant. Maynard is a former Mr. Universe, six feet tall and 225 pounds, with a forty-four-inch chest and arms like most football player's thighs. The guy is built like the side of a ship, and the local double we'd hired didn't even come close to matching Earl's monumental proportions.

It looked like Earl Maynard would have to do his own underwater stunts, after all. We were out on *Moby II* when this cosmic revelation hit us—two days ago. Two days before that key underwater approach scene was scheduled to be filmed.

In the best frantic Hollywood style, we immediately got a phone line to Peter Island and from there to Los Angeles and Columbia V.P. John Veitch, who performed heroically. John issued an all-points-bulletin for Earl, who was out of town at the time, tracked him down, and bundled him onto a plane for San Juan. Within thirty-six hours our hulking heavy was on Peter Island, taking a cram diving course in that big pool where the rest of us old salts had begun our diving careers. Earl looked stiff and awkward in the water and seemed none too fond of it, but we foolishly assume that a big athletic type like him would master diving automatically.

And today, because of our impatience, Earl was deemed ready to go—by this time, in all fairness to Earl, if he was underwater and still breathing it was good enough for us—whisked out of the pool and onto *Moby II*. Although not given adequate training time he was given detailed instructions in the skull session this morning. Earl had no complex moves; just a long, straight swim down to the camera, at which point he would turn left and enter the hull of the ship. End of shot.

So the shot's set up by the underwater lighting guys, and Earl is stationed at his mark alongside the ship about thirty yards away. Peter Yates gives the "action" signal, and Earl starts swimming, pumping along so comically he looks like a crazed circus unicyclist. But he doesn't stop and turn left when he reaches the cameras; he just keeps right on going, over Giddings, Waterman, and Nicklin's heads and off into the green mist beyond. As he passes, everyone sees the most terrified, glassy-eyed look on this big bruiser's face they've ever seen on any novice diver, anywhere. Earl seems petrified; literally blind with fear, and all he can do is just keep pumping and swimming. If two crew members hadn't zipped after him and grabbed his flipper and shaken him out of it, he'd probably be somewhere off the coast of Cuba by now. The crew members bring Earl back to his mark, go through his move for him, and he nods, OK, he's got it this time. The cameras roll. Earl starts swimming. And he doesn't turn left. He just keeps swimming into the great green beyond until he's yanked back again.

This time the team takes Earl back onto *Moby II* and goes over his move again on the blackboard.

Everything is diagrammed and Earl understands perfectly. Back down for another take. The cameras roll, and Earl comes along, and everyone holds their breath—but Earl is as glassy-eyed as ever and *again* he goes right over everyone's heads bound for Cuba or wherever the hell he's pointed. By this time the team must have considered just letting Earl keep on swimming, but they dutifully hauled him back. The stunt wasn't attempted again, though. By this time it was painfully obvious that Earl would need more time, lots more time, to master diving, and we'd have to somehow do his scenes later in the ocean off Bermuda.

Suddenly our scheduled departure for Bermuda looms uncomfortably close. Not that we all aren't chomping at the bit to get off Peter Island. But we want to make sure we get as much underwater footage as possible, here and now—because once we bid farewell to the British Virgins, we won't be coming back for pick-ups. So we've decided to overlap the production. That way, we can continue our underwater filming in BVI for an extra week while simultaneously beginning surface filming in Bermuda. Al Giddings and Stan Waterman, after consultation with Yates, will direct the rest of the second unit underwater BVI filming with their "Gorillas" and of course, Yates' storyboards.

Bisset, who planned to go back to Los Angeles for a break before rejoining the production in Bermuda, is by now so engrossed in her underwater exploits that she insists on staying an additional day to do some extra angles and pick-ups. Jackie is really into the character of Gail now, too; so much so that yesterday she inadvertently caused yet another scary moment in the deep for Nick Nolte.

Remember Percy the Eel, and the two scenes which must establish him before he chomps down on Cloche? Well, one of them occurs right at the beginning of the film. Gail is snooping around the exterior of the *Goliath* when she happens on a hole (Percy's hole, but she doesn't know that) and spots something glittery inside. She reaches her prodding stick in, and it's suddenly grabbed inside by the unseen eel. The stick is slung around Gail's wrist and she can't break free—she's caught, tumbling around in utter disorientation and panic. Using her wits, Gail finally removes the mouthpiece from her mouth and shoots a stream of air into the hole, startling the unseen creature into dropping her now-mangled stick. Gail doesn't hang around to find out what it was; she bolts to the surface. David, exploring another part of the wreck, doesn't know what's happened, but when he sees Gail he shoots up after her, grabbing her flipper to slow her too rapid ascent. In her terror Gail thinks that whatever has hold of her flipper now is the thing that grabbed her stick just moments before, and she starts flailing around frantically trying to shake free.

Jackie flailed, all right—a little too frantically. She was so involved that one of her wild kicks and thrusts smashed Nick's regulator. Suddenly Nick had a useless piece of equipment in his mouth and no air to breathe sixty feet down. He quickly began to rise toward the surface after Jackie. Three Gorillas immediately offered Nick their mouthpieces, and he buddy-breathed to the surface with one of them. It was a harrowing moment, but Nick stayed cool as always, and the smashed mouthpiece incident was so dramatic when we later saw it in the dailies tonight that it was written right into the film.

A last hurrah party was held tonight at Guber Gulch for what remains of cast and crew. The grub consisted of everything left in our refrigerator, including what was left of some New York deli cuisine we'd smuggled in with a prop shipment a few weeks ago. Jackie and Nick were alone up at Crow's Nest, and came in looking very pleased with each other long after the exhausted crew had said their goodnights. They'd been going over the script and had come up with several nice touches. In spite of the inevitable speculation to the contrary, their friendship doesn't seem to have turned them into lovers. But Jackie and Nick are working together beautifully, and their shared experiences in the deep has formed a real bond between them.

It's that way with the whole company. Our diving record is proof of the superb teamwork that has evolved over the weeks. When he toted up the numbers, Denny Breese was amazed. With the 1,465 dives we'd made in all over thirty-five consecutive days, the usual occurrence of the bends would be something like 10 percent, or 14 cases, with about three being fairly serious. But we didn't experience a single case! We've had our share of scares, but not one member of the company, novice or veteran diver, has been hurt.

July 25

Landlubbing Hollywood types have learned all about diving; underwater filmmakers have learned all about making Hollywood movies; Al Giddings' Petermars have functioned without a hitch. And we have authentic footage of our stars diving in the Caribbean deep to show for our grueling, exhilarating first month of filming. The underwater team and the Hollywood team have won each other's admiration and respect during our time in BVI . . . and each other's friendship, too. Though it's only for a week, we hate saying good-bye to Giddings, Waterman, and the Gorillas. But there's plenty of work to be done yet. So while our underwater team continues immortalizing the *Rhone* over, under, around, and through, the first unit is packing up, shipping out, and going on to the next phase of filming *The Deep* in Bermuda.

7
B-DAY: LAND AT LAST!

~~~~~~

After our long weeks on Peter Island, even quaint Bermuda is, to us, a culture shock of some magnitude. All of a sudden, everywhere we look, there are streets! Cars! Houses! And best of all, people! This tiny, isolated island country seems like a bustling metropolis to our stimuli-starved eyeballs. Actually, even Bermuda's little capital city of Hamilton, while bustling, can hardly be called a metropolis, but then Bermuda can hardly be called a country. It's much more like a large village. But after stumbling off those tourist-filled jets from New York, the last and quickest leg of our wearying long haul from Peter Island, all we know is that this lovely island—now comfortably basking in the full flush of summer— looks damn good to us.

At a mere twenty-two miles long and an average of one mile wide, water is almost everywhere you look in Bermuda. The South Shore is one gorgeous pink beach after another, all overlooking that vast turquoise sea. Along the winding north coast runs Harbour Road, just as beautiful as South Shore Road except that its views run to picturesque harbors complete with peaceful armadas of bobbing boats and the sight of Hamilton twinkling across the water. In between, on either side of (naturally) Middle Road, Bermuda looks like a gorgeous botanical garden gone mad. And the rainbow-colored Bermudian houses fit right into this picture postcard of a landscape, nestling cozily amid the lush greenery like Easter eggs in a bed of moss. All in all, Bermuda has such a clean, bright, almost unnaturally colorful beauty that it inspired our Production

Designer Tony Masters to sputter bemusedly, on an early location recce, "It's hard to find locations that look *real* here—this whole place looks like one giant movie set!"

Well, now that the first unit has landed in Bermuda, the whole place just about is.

The seven larger islands (out of a total 138) that make up the main landmass of the "island" of Bermuda are all linked by bridge or causeway, and together they form a long, narrow fishhook shape running east and west. Months before on our scouting trips we'd snooped over every gorgeous square foot and chosen several locations for *The Deep*'s various surface scenes. On several of these locations, sets have already sprouted which change the whole character of the landscape. A barren little handful of sand and rock called Coney Island has become the setting for our own version of St. David's Lighthouse. Now perched on a recently empty hill, Treece's home is a brand new weatherbeaten structure with a bright red tower and a dilapidated waterside dock, all looking as if they have been there for decades. A bare, high cliff overlooking a narrow coral-strewn beach now sports a huge red steel-and-fiberglass elevator—our "Orange Grove" lift. Dotted all over Bermuda are the many other locations that we'll be hopping restlessly back and forth between in the long months to come.

Production headquarters have been set up clear at the island's western tip, in the Dockyard, a fortress-like group of massive stone buildings with its own fascinating history. Bermuda, of course, is a British colony, and over a hundred years ago the Royal Navy decided that their little island preserve was the perfect place for a strategic base to be "The Gibraltar of the West." To build the mighty stronghold they had in mind, the Navy shipped 9,000 English convicts and untold tons of English stone to Bermuda, and thus was the Dockyard built over a period of forty years. It proved to be every bit as useful as its builders had foreseen, an important base for both U.S. and British forces in the various skirmishes (like World War I and II) which the world has seen since its construction.

In the 1950's the Dockyard was more or less closed down, and most of those massive stone buildings were just lying around, begging to be turned into a mid-Atlantic movie studio by the likes of us. So that's just what we've done. *The Deep,* while not the Navy, is one determined, fast-moving army, and we quickly took over this perfect location as headquarters. A small administrative complex houses our offices, complete with fluorescent lights; cluttered desks; phones ringing incessantly; IBM typewriters clattering away; and even a huge war map of Bermuda with little colored flags to indicate our various locations throughout the island. And an English stone's throw away, carpentry, plaster, and paint shops are all going strong under the guidance of construction supervisor Dick Frift. A large room in the old bell tower building has become our screening room. Two huge shipbuilding warehouses that once stored sails now house two key interior sets: Treece's house on Sound Stage One, and, next door, David and Gail's bungalow at the Orange Grove, perfect down to the last gold-framed watercolor.

Across the way from our offices, suave British propmaster Graham Sumner oversees a complete prop shop, and Special Effects, headed by Ira Anderson, Jr., is semipermanently parked nearby. Now, some folks take their own professional equipment with them wherever they go—which is easy when you're the piccolo player with the local symphony. It's not so easy when you're the special effects man on a multi-million dollar location shoot and you need your very own monster special effects truck, the size of which puts a Bekins van to shame, to do your thing. Ira's van—the largest such set-up in the world—could not very comfortably make the trip in the DC-10 he himself arrived on; it had to be driven across the country from California to New York, where it was loaded onto a huge ship and boated down to Bermuda. That headache pointed up yet another advantage to the Dockyard. In addition to being spacious, secluded, sturdy, and empty, it's also, well, a dockyard, and the incredible amounts of equipment we have to move into Bermuda can be unloaded right off ships from New York practically at our doorstep. In addition to the myriad of things we'll need for filming and goodies like shipments of explosives for our many special effects, every single piece of lumber, metal tubing, pipe, wire, and electronics that we used to build our sets had to be brought to Bermuda this way. Once they got here, our English construction team had to rebuild old Bermuda buses to carry it all around in, since Bermuda doesn't have any trucks large enough.

All of this activity is going on in a total area of only twenty square miles or so, across which, on any U.S. freeway at a good time, you'd get in twenty-five minutes or so. But on Bermuda, there are no freeways, and the winding country roads which are its only thoroughfares have a strictly enforced speed limit of twenty miles per hour. That's aggravating enough for those of us used to whizzing along great stretches of freeway at fifty-five miles per hour. Consider the plight, then, of British Art Director Jack Maxstead, who loves to drive fast, lives for the time each year when he can barrel down the European freeways to his vacation house in Malta. He's going stir-crazy crawling along the Bermuda roads.

But not only is moving fast more fun, it also gets you wherever you're going faster. At twenty mph, you don't get anywhere fast . . . especially in Bermuda. We often have to change locations in mid-day because the weather gets temperamental. That means scurrying to load our huge vehicles with tons of equipment, only to have to rumble ponderously along the narrow roads, like the Allied Forces entering rural France, before pulling up to our new location over an hour later and trying to save what was left of the day.

As you can well imagine, *The Deep,* with its trucks and artillery and towering new edifices and squawking walkie-talkies, is nothing less than a full-fledged occupation of Bermuda, albeit a benign one. The Bermudians have reacted to our presence like any group of people under siege: they try to ignore us. Oh, they're fascinated, all right, but you couldn't have pried an admission of interest from a Bermudian under intense interrogation by klieg light. No, as far as they're concerned, movie stars are just folks, movies are just something to do when it's too rough to go sailing, and everything after *The Deep*'s arrival is precisely the same as before.

But, truly, it's anything but. We're the center of interest in Bermuda, and all eyes are upon us, voluntarily or not. Letting it be known that you work on *The Deep,* or, better yet, wearing a "Deep" T-shirt, is an instant conversation-opener—and favor-getter—all over the island. In fact, those T-shirts have become a precious commodity. Though kept in the office under lock and key, they have a way of mysteriously disappearing and reappearing on the backs of non-staffers who are not even remotely involved in the production. And those who can't get an authentic "Deep" T-shirt by begging, borrowing, or stealing can now satisfy their craving with a quickie rip-off version that features a Bisset-like silhouette beneath the exhortation, "Peep the Deep."

Still, the initial reaction of the Bermudians is understandable. They know they live in paradise, or about as close as you're likely to get in this life, and they share their good fortune with each other and tourists alike. But we are something else altogether. It's as if a horde of paparazzi had descended on them as they lounged in their own backyards, clicking off mysterious, possibly unflattering snapshots that they wouldn't see for years, if at all. So, for a while at least, they're wary.

August 5

If the locals are trying like mad to play it cool, the thousands of vacationers they're currently sharing their island with have no shame. On locations, every chubby, sunburned American tourist on the island seems to turn up, wandering into frame, stepping on cables, and grabbing Nick Nolte to pose for pictures with his arm around the little woman. Even back in our Dockyard offices, which we thought so secluded, we can't escape. Tourists visiting the Bermuda Maritime Museum across the way discover *The Deep*. They stare in fascination at the placard over our office's front door like it's a magical incantation. They ignore sternly worded signs and walk right into Treece's interior to rearrange the props which our Academy Award-winning set decorator Vernon Dixon (*Barry Lyndon, Nicholas and Alexandra, Dr. Zhivago*) had placed so carefully. Mild-mannered Vernon caught one in the act, and practically tore his head off.

The fishbowl atmosphere follows us each evening right off the set and into the Southampton Princess Hotel where the team is headquartered. The Princess is just like any huge, modern hotel anywhere: luxurious, convenient, monolithic, and bland—and for us, not only disastrously expensive but utterly without privacy. In the hotel lobby, the management has proudly placed a large placard proclaiming the Princess as "Home of The Deep!" It is, and will remain so for publicity purposes, press and visitor housing. But most "Deepers" have quickly tired of being constantly pounced on by tourists all playing the identical game of Twenty Questions, and many are already making plans to move to cozier, more private, and cheaper accommodations.

But that will have to come later. Even if you entrust your house-hunting to a real estate agent (many of us have, and regret it for the soaring rents we've ended up paying), looking for a place takes time. Of that commodity, we have precious little to spare. No sooner had we landed in Bermuda than we had to get our Cricket Match scene together—fast.

The Bermuda Cup Match has been a tradition on the island for seventy-five years. This year, it will also serve as the inspired setting for a new scene Peter Benchley has written for the film: a tense confrontation during which Romer Treece buys time to bring up the morphine from the *Goliath* by pretending he'll sell it to Cloche. The Match—vividly, typically Bermudian—is a perfect backdrop, but it also promises to be a headache to shoot because the Cup Match is the biggest sports event on the island, attracting approximately 20,000 locals for the fun. In fact, the Match is a national holiday for everyone but the officials, and for them, it's a logistical nightmare. For a feature film crew to be present on top of the regular annual madness meant days of getting everything squared away on both sides so it would all be ready when the game began. There were permits to be obtained; the field had to be checked out for lighting and sound; Director Peter Yates huddled with Cinematographer Chris Challis and wanted a full rehearsal with Lou Gosset and Robert Shaw. Well, Cloche was bright-eyed, cooperative, and ready to go—but hero Treece threw us a real curve ball this afternoon, just before the game.

Yep, our Romer Treece inadvertently almost blew our one chance to capture the Cup Match for *The Deep,* as Robert Shaw made his way down the DC-10 gangplank on his arrival at Bermuda Airport yesterday. With a grin on his face, Shaw announced: "Jay (Virginia Jansen) and I have decided to get married—today!" Now, Virginia Jansen is a wonderful woman, and the merger had everybody's blessings, but the timing left a little something to be desired. Congratulations, Robert! We hope the two of you will be very happy. Okay, all is forgiven. And can we get this over with fairly quickly, please, so we can get ready to film tomorrow?

Immediately *The Deep* was enlisted to cut through not only its own red tape, but the red tape that surrounds holy matrimony in Bermuda like it does everywhere else. Again official papers were flying like confetti. Only this time they were Shaw's birth certificate; Virginia's nationality papers; divorce decrees; a death certificate for Mary Ure, Shaw's late wife. At last all these were assembled under a crisp, new Bermudian marriage license, and Robert and Virginia were married at the magistrate's office in Hamilton, with A.D. Derek Cracknell serving as witness. We never did manage to rehearse, but there we were at the Cricket Match bright and early this morning to begin filming. After all, the

Bermudians, no matter how kindly disposed toward *The Deep*, weren't about to delay their most important sports event of the year so that one of our cast could have a honeymoon.

August 6

The Cup Match, played between St. George's and Somerset, (the eastern- and westernmost two of the nine parishes, or regional divisions, of Bermuda), is something like land-locked baseball played over a period of two full days. There's a batting team and a field team, and the object is to get nine wickets. All in all, it's about as exciting as watching paint dry, but the Bermudians love it. The game itself is rather decorous, but the Match has a lively carnival atmosphere. Booths and tents crowd the paths surrounding the field; liquor flows freely; fans don their wildest clothes and most raucous spirits for the event.

Happily, most were so pleasantly wasted that they took no notice of our hand-held cameras as we worked our way through the crowd. Some did dart up to shake Robert Shaw's hand, but even that worked perfectly, since, as Romer Treece, he's known and accorded respect by everyone on the island.

Although they've only got three theaters on the entire island and movies arrive one or two years after they've come and gone in the States (*Jaws* is only now breaking here), the Bermudians know enough to be star-struck like anyone else. Whenever we need extras we have no shortage of applicants, eagerly dressed in the showy clothes of contestants on *Let's Make a Deal*. The sound is a grab-bag of yells, shouts, and reggae music drifting through the air, which makes a great background but also ensures that we'll have to redo the dialogue tracks later. But over the game's two days, plus one extra day of controlled filming in the then-deserted stadium while workers begin the monumental task of cleaning up, we'll get our Cricket Match scene in the can.

Already, after just a few days in Bermuda, our Peter Island experience seems very far away. But it isn't over yet. Our underwater team is still working on the *Rhone,* but we have no idea what they're getting on film: We've seen no new footage since coming to Bermuda. Now we're comparatively just a hop and a skip from the New York lab, but rushes still have to go through the same dreary customs rigamarole back and forth, so they'll continue to come in four or five days late throughout our months in Bermuda.

We don't really want to pull the team out of BVI just to come and twiddle their water-wrinkled thumbs while we complete our underwater set for filming. But a rumored impending air controller's strike in New York threatens to slow down their arrival in Bermuda uncontrollably. That's an even more harrowing prospect, since it would throw everything else in our already strained shooting schedule off. So today we called Al on Peter Island and asked him to pull the Gorillas out a day early.

8
LOADING THE B.U.S.

~~~~~~

Now we're in a special crunch. We're down to the wire trying to get our underwater set built, assembled, dressed, filled with water and fish and finalized for filming. To put it in the Filmworkese of our own early memos, we have a B.U.S. to get rolling.

Already an incredible amount of work has been done. The last time I saw our site, it was a parched, rocky, undistinguished hill of coral overlooking the ocean, reachable only up a torturously steep and narrow pebble-strewn road. Since then, bulldozers, cranes, thousands of pounds of equipment and dozens of men have made that journey up the hill. A huge excavation —120 feet in diameter and thirty feet deep—was clawed out of the rock in 100–plus degree heat. Meanwhile, Art Director Terry Ackland-Snow had supervised the construction of the set itself—a huge creation of metal framing, fiberglass, and concrete with seventeen separate chambers, including the moray eel's lair and the new *Grifon* chamber Tony had created below. The *Goliath* set was so large it had to be built in separate sections, lowered in by crane, and mounted together later in the site.

But first, the entire lining of the site had to be sealed with urethane foam. No one was completely sure that the porous coral rock would retain the one million gallons of sea water it would take to fill the set, and no one was about to take the chance. The job was Carlos Machado's, and he performed heroically.

Urethane foam is a nightmare to work with. Made by combining two chemicals in a special machine, it's so dangerous—combustible *and* reeking with poisonous fumes—that Carlos had to drive its ingredients across country himself, and personally supervise their shipping from New York to Bermuda. That left Carlos three weeks behind his original two-week application schedule with exactly six days to cover the entire surface of the set with two separate layers of this stuff. Carlos and foreman Emmet Jones donned special protective suits against the toxic fumes, and the fire department stood by as they began spraying by the first rays of dawn one morning till it was too dark to see the spray gun that night. The next morning they were back at it again, and the next. Together they applied 15,000 pounds of foam from thirty huge drums, and, incredibly, got the job done on target.

By this time, Carlos and Emmet were probably ready to collapse on their own urethane handiwork, but it was time to get out of the way. "*Rhone* coming through!" Here comes the *Rhone* set now, this huge artificial recreation of a shipwreck hundreds of miles away taking form in a gigantic urethane-lined cereal bowl of a site on a dusty, rocky Bermuda hill. The set was lowered down in sections, a task again requiring an entire corps of workers, a large amount of equipment, and a huge amount of care. Finally in place, each piece had to be anchored down with a series of heavy pipes so it would stay put and not come bobbing to the surface like a gargantuan rubber duck when the site was filled.

Every detail is an intricate chore. Sand to line certain key sections of the set, for example. But not just plain old sand. It must be immaculately clean sand, yet heavy enough to settle fast between takes or else precious hours would be lost when filming began. The only sand that meets those requirements is the coral sand that lays at the bottom of the ocean floor—eight miles off the coast. So Kym Murphy, our marine biologist, went out to get it—500 sacks at 100 pounds each, brought up from the sea floor and back to the site.

The pumps that Kym had designed and helped in-

stall were then activated. Operating only during in-
coming tide to ensure cleaner water, they had to draw
it up a thirty-five-foot rise from sea level before forcing
it through a filtration system and into the set. Real,
clean salt water began to spew furiously into the site,
and just as Kym had predicted, it lapped up a million
gallons' worth in just twelve hours. But already there's
trouble. The water is still cloudy from all the turbulence, which was expected. But the water level is dropping, which was not. The pumps continue to pump and
replace the water as needed. But without a stable water line we can't get everything else completed, and
there are still plenty of items left on our BUS
schedule.

While the team charged with the construction of our
underwater set struggles to keep their heads above water, the land unit is trying valiantly to complete some
key surface filming. Working on land is both a respite
and a chance to boost morale by accomplishing some
good solid work done with our collective feet planted
on the good solid ground. But we have our share of
headaches on terra firma already.

We had planned on spending all of today filming in
the newly completed interior of Treece's house on
Sound Stage One at the Dockyard. Thanks to Tony
Masters and Construction Supervisor Dick Frift, the
layout and the look of Treece's rooms were just right.
And to dress them, Set Decorator Vernon Dixon had
obtained an assortment of furniture and knicknacks
that was nothing short of extraordinary, all painstakingly hunted down and gathered from local sources in
what amounts to a prize feat of artistic detective work.
Rich old mahogany furniture, old-fashioned tole lamps,
musty old books, shelves full of *National Geographics,*
mysterious little bottles of liquid, examination tools,
and encrusted bottles all fill the set in a carefully controlled clutter that looks as if it had accumulated over
twenty years instead of barely two months, and speaks
volumes about our mysterious hero.

The set is a masterpiece, all right, but we just discovered that the old English stone which retains cool damp air also retains the heat from the huge lights needed for filming much too well. The temperature shot up to over 100 degrees, and our actors were soon dripping with sweat. While we did get some shots in, it's obvious that if we want to spare our stars from heat prostration from now on we'll have to wait for cooler weather, or get some fans in there (air conditioning is out of the question for financial reasons), or do something else to make that set livable that was not going to get done this afternoon.

Now there's the case of the Orange Grove elevator.

Over at Marley Beach on Bermuda's South Shore, a marvel of engineering has been erected. The Orange Grove elevator Peter Benchley concocted on paper has now materialized into a slender 113-foot lift rising straight up the side of a cliff. Our brilliant odd-couple team of Masters and Maxstead has designed this thing to look like it's been standing since the 1920's, with exposed structure and ornamental "metalwork" (actually molded fiberglass) throughout.

Construction Supervisor Dick Frift made it happen. Dick hired a local to build the elevator. It was no easy task. The elevator could not be supported at all by the soft limestone cliffside rock, and it had to be anchored at the bottom and secured at the top to a large block of concrete hauled over just for that purpose, with safety wires laced throughout the structure to keep it from bending. The elevator had to look good, it had to be safe for our actors, it had to really work, and it had to do all these things from the minute we'd begin filming on it.

Now, we didn't go to all this trouble just for the scene early in the book where David and Gail emerge from the ocean and go up the lift to their cottage to fool around and get ready for dinner. Not for $80,000. Early on, it was a case of either lose the elevator or make it more useful, and after much debating, we chose the latter. The Orange Grove elevator is a perfectly cinematic, scarily precipitous thing for David to have to clamber up after his night dive with Treece when he suddenly realizes that back at the cottage, Gail is in danger. And what better place to stage a fight with Cloche's men? The scene as now written is suspenseful as all hell—David tangles with Cloche's heavies under cover of darkness on this huge steel structure dozens of feet above the beach.

That will all be shot later, though. First we want to establish the Orange Grove elevator working in the background during the earlier day scene, now rewritten to include David and Gail's first fateful encounter with Slake, the Orange Grove boatman who moonlights for the nefarious Cloche. It's a relatively simple scene, and we'd wanted to get it completed during our first week in Bermuda. To do that, of course, we needed our Orange Grove elevator completed on time.

There is something called "Bermuda time," which the following anecdote may help to illustrate. Rita Harthorn, one of the production secretaries in our company, is an American now living in Bermuda. She had a date with a Bermudian fellow for 9 o'clock one Thursday night. She got all dressed up, 9 o'clock comes and goes, and it gradually became apparent that her date was not coming. Rita shrugged and went to bed and that was that. Fine.

One week to the minute later, next Thursday night at 9 o'clock, the doorbell rang. Rita went to the door and there, standing expectantly with a big grin on his face, was her long-lost date. Rita smiled wryly. "Don't you think you're a bit late?"

"What's the matter?" her date replied. "I said 9 o'clock, didn't I?"

And that is Bermuda time, a kind of mañana mentality that easily rivals the more publicized Mexican variety. One hour, one day, one week—as long as it gets done more or less when you want it—what's the difference? It makes a cute story, but when you're making a feature film you avoid "more or less" schedules like the plague. Delays inevitably come along no matter what you do, but at $35,000 a day, why lay out a welcome-mat for them?

August 12

Now, 99 percent of the Bermudian labor we'd hired to work on the film was efficient and hardworking. But there was 1 percent with this more relaxed attitude toward life, and he was in charge of our Orange Grove elevator. Our contractor had apparently built his organization from the ground up on Bermuda time, and he was now seemingly intent on building our elevator from the ground up in much the same way. Poor Dick Frift, who prefers to speak softly and doesn't like to have to wield big sticks, had to badger the contractor continually to keep pace as he fell days, then weeks behind schedule. Finally, the elevator was finished. We loaded up this morning and went out to film on it, hoping above all to get that crucial establishing shot of Jackie and Nick walking up the beach as, in the background, some bathers get into the elevator car and start up the cliff.

We'd completed maybe two shots, when at 2 P.M. the elevator breaks down. Grinds to a halt. Won't move. This contractor was called in a panic, and he assures us that he'll get to it sometime in the next few days, how does that sound? You'll get to it now, Or Else, was Dick's reply, and they get out to Marley Beach on Hollywood time for once: fast. We kept shooting and Yates managed to get everything he needed. The company moved out in the afternoon and on to other shots on other sets, leaving the contractor and his crew to their labors. We'd be back for later scenes and the elevator had better run perfectly.

Had Swann's workers, perched up on that elevator, looked way out onto the horizon, they might have spotted a small flotilla of boats on which, far out to sea, work on our underwater set was still going on. Divers have been going out for days to explore some of Bermuda's several hundred shipwrecks for the authentic props yet needed to dress our *Goliath*.

Meanwhile, Kym Murphy and some of the guys went fishing.

"Going fishing" for our underwater set was no leisurely outing. Murphy, along with Carlos Machado and incredibly knowledgeable and helpful Teddy Tucker, actually have to dive to find the types of fish we need, which have to match those found on the *Rhone,* 1500 miles south, because they are only to be found, like those on the *Rhone,* in sixty or more feet of water. Fish are delicate creatures and can easily go into fatal shock when caught. So they have to be tranquilized with Quinaldine, a knock-out drug, and then placed in special bags.

When fish are caught at the lower depths and then brought up, they can suffer an embolism from expanding air in their air bladders just as a human being can in his lungs. Fish are capable of inflating and deflating their air bags at will, but in captivity they'll often refuse to do so and, like little marine kamikazes, would just as soon blow themselves to smithereens as be captured. So a diver hovering at thirty feet must take the fish from the diver rising from sixty feet and "bleed" the fish of excess air with a hypodermic needle. Near the surface, this process is repeated.

The fish are put into holding tanks on Tucker's boat, and then, at the end of the day, transferred to a fenced-off live habitat in the sea near Tucker's dock. Each day Teddy or his wife Edna feed the fish until their condition stabilizes. Then they're collected, Quinaldined again, put into holding tanks once more, and trucked up to the underwater set, where they're released in the shallow end. As they come out of their stupor, our fish naturally gravitate toward their new home—the protective nooks and crannies of the *Goliath* set.

Seagoing Gorillas, too, have been gravitating in the same direction. Giddings and the underwater team have moved out from Peter Island. Just packing everything up took a good day and a half. And anyone who's ever grumbled as they waited in a crowded airport for their little avocado-green Samsonite to come around

the bend would do well to consider Al Giddings vying
for conveyor-belt space at good old San Juan Airport
—waiting for *eighty-eight* separate crates of equipment,
three of them carrying his beautiful cameras, to emerge
from some DC-3's steel belly.

The underwater team finally made it to Bermuda today, and, though exhausted, they were eager to see
their watery home for the next six weeks. Soon they
were up at the underwater set preparing for a dive.
As eager as they were, I was nervous. Here were divers
who'd explored and filmed in oceans the world over,
about to work for the first time in what is, after all, a
Hollywood set. It's a masterpiece by Hollywood stan-
dards, but I was secretly afraid that our team would
be less than overwhelmed by it.

Well, they went crazy. They were like kids again,
playing with the greatest toy in the world. The Gorillas
swam all through our set's many nooks and crannies,
in and out, over and over, marveling at the sheer scale
and accuracy of it. The life-sized model holds all the
fascinations of the real thing for them, and around it,
the dish shape of the site moves off into visual in-
finity just as Tony Masters had intended, making it look
very much like the real ocean. "Wow!" "Terrific!"
"Incredible!" They couldn't say enough in its praise.
Not only are they looking forward to working in the
set—their fresh optimism is a sorely needed tonic for
the rest of us. "Less than one percent of even the
diving community will be able to tell where the real
Rhone leaves off and that set begins," Al declared
upon surfacing. Meaning, natch, that non-diving audiences will be happily oblivious and spellbound
throughout.

But not everything is rosy yet, by any means. The
set continues to lose water at the rate of 200,000 gallons a day. Where in the world is it going? Chuck
Nicklin dove to find out what's going on—and almost
lost a hand as it got sucked down an open stanchion
pipe on the set bottom.

Some of the pipes which support the set had been

driven past the urethane lining and were leaking water into the coral bed below. The turbulence of the water coming in to replace it accounts for our set's continued cloudiness. The underwater team plugged as many open pipes as they could reach with wooden blocks, greatly reducing the leakage but not stemming it completely. However, Kym Murphy assures us that the pumps will continue to replace the lost water, and that it will make for a better, less stagnant biological environment to have some fresh sea water coming in daily.

Having already sprung several slow leaks was bad enough, but what, we wondered, if the porous coral beneath gives way? Thank God for small favors; we learned that leaking water has absolutely no effect on the rocky base on which our set is built. Had it been earth, it would have collapsed in the space of a week!

Topside, work has continued on the various structures we'll need around the set itself. A long, tarpaulin-covered gangplank has been built to provide cool working and storage space right over the site. Several shacks have sprung up to house things like camera equipment, lighting, and underwater special effects materials. A series of air-conditioned dressing rooms have been set up along the side. At the set's far, deep end, a huge tent has been erected, with long tables and dozens of chairs to provide a lunch area for the team. And at the shallow end, a small press arcade has carefully been constructed for the journalists that will soon descend on us. What looks to the casual observer like a comfortable little gazebo with chairs, early press clippings, and a small 3-D model of the underwater set is the result of hours and hours of planning. Here, even more than in BVI, it's vital that the press really understand what our shoot is all about.

Although even from the surface it's an exotic sight, all the action still is, or will be, on the inside, and the press can't possibly get a real feeling for what's going on unless they actually go down there. Hopefully, it won't be too difficult to persuade several journalists into the set, and, on that optimistic assumption, we've laid in a special supply of diving gear marked "PRESS."

The underwater set is rapidly nearing the time when we'll begin filming in it. We'll be plunging in to see just how closely it lives up to our sky-high expectations very soon. We're counting on the set to provide us with the control needed to accomplish all the close-up underwater filming still to be done: the long underwater sequences with our stars and the numerous complicated "gags," or special-effects stunts, orchestrated around the story's elements: the characters, the wreck itself, and that big, mean moray eel.

August 16

We squeezed in one last surface shoot before beginning in our underwater set.

The scene in which Cloche first comes upon David and Gail at the Orange Grove restaurant is an important one. It immediately sets up the tension of *The Deep*, showing the carefree, glossy tourist world in which David and Gail move until the sudden, irrevocable intrusion of Cloche, the evil presence who will dog and threaten them till the very end of the story. It's a short scene, and an ostensibly simple one, but it has a lot to accomplish, efficiently and gracefully.

With all that in mind, we prepared for our Orange Grove scene. A location was found and "dressed", Jackie and Nick and Lou were costumed, several bands were auditioned to play music in the background, and several eager extras were found to dance to it. Our actors were rehearsed, and, since it's a night scene, the cameras began to roll at seven o'clock last evening.

Yates continued on through drizzle and severely tired spirits of the local extras till the crack of dawn. By that time, both the company and eager extras just wanted to escape and go crash somewhere more than anything in the world.

So at 6 A.M. on this dreary morning, along with the sun dawned the realization that it's time to go back to the Deep. Our B.U.S. is ready for boarding—and just in time, too: Percy is on his way.

9
IT'S A MORAY, NOT AMORÉ

August 18

The DC–10 made a flawless touchdown at Bermuda International Airport. Inside, in his own long, wooden crate, Percy III—our twelve-foot "rigid" Percy—lay in traction on a series of special slings to keep him from bumping around. His two hydraulic brothers are still in incubation back in Walter Stones' garage, being readied for their own trips to Bermuda in a few weeks' time.

Percy had just about made it through Bermuda Customs, protectively escorted by Peter Lake, when a bouncy, gray-haired customs employee insisted on a peek. She opened Percy's crate up a crack and shrieked, "I wouldn't get into the water with *that!*" She'll never have to, but those words were music to our ears. Percy was hustled out of the airport and into a covered truck, whisked clear across the island to our underwater set, and carefully unloaded. The human telegraph quickly spread the word of his arrival, and several of us gathered around for the great unveiling. Ira Anderson and Charlie Spurgeon quickly removed the screws that held down the crate's cover. We held our breath. The top was raised as reverently as the cover of Dracula's crypt . . .

This boy needs some work. Percy's color is terrible; his skin looks like it was dropped into Campbell's split pea soup. Those beady glass eyes of his are much too glassy. If Percy's going to make a splash on screen, he's got to get some quick cosmetic surgery and plenty of make-up. We're in big trouble.

Carlos Machado and Eddie Lima zipped over to the Bermuda aquarium and studied our real, green, seven-foot eel at close range, making notes on new eyes for Percy and a two-tone paint job that would make his rubber hide look like nature's own handiwork. Just revitalized, the new improved Percy III was lowered into his very own lair in our underwater set for a visual test. Giddings and Waterman examined him underwater like a couple of medical specialists going over a renowned patient. This time Percy got a clean bill of health. In fact, he looks frighteningly authentic to every member of our underwater team—and all of them have had encounters with the real thing. When Percy is properly placed in his carefully lit eel hole, the effect should be electrifying.

It had better be. Percy III will be the first of our moray eels showing his snout on screen, and he has to be convincingly established as a terrifying creature right away. Otherwise, we'll be risking giggles and guffaws when Percy I and II take over for their climactic scene with Cloche. We've worked this whole thing out very carefully. Gail's tangle with the unseen eel comes first, so that the audience knows that *something* is in that hole, but not quite what it is. In this scene with Percy III, there will be no uncertainty.

David and Treece are down at the wreck during their first night dive together. Treece is laying explosives to blow the *Goliath* and its munitions and morphine cargo sky high, and David is unwittingly messing around near the eel hole. He sees a large, photogenic fish, but by the time he gets ready to take a picture of it, only the ragged head of the fish floats eerily in front of him. Puzzled, David scans the area with his lamp cautiously, and *wham!* Percy zips across the screen like a bolt of lightning directly at him. David is flung back toward an ancient ladder in the hold and is caught on its broken rungs. His camera tumbles out of his hands; the strobe shorts and starts flashing sporadically, illuminating David and the eel in an eerie dance of light. Then the strobe begins to die—and David is trapped in the dark with Percy.

The moments seem to last forever until Treece comes to the rescue, and the two of them respectfully watch as the giant eel retreats back into his hole.

The entire sequence will last less than a minute, but it must be built of a whole series of separate shots. David spotting the fish. David getting ready to take its picture. The ragged fish head now floating before him. Percy whipping across the screen. David jumping back and getting caught on the ladder rung. The camera tumbling out of his hands, and its strobe flashing to provide that spooky light—a separate special effect. Shots of our real eel swimming around in a special half-size set . . . That's only a small portion of the individual shots needed, not to mention a few angles of every shot, and a few takes of every angle.

Not only do we have to get all of this in the can, but all of it has to cut together. Everything—lighting, angles, eel movements—must be perfectly matched or the scene just will not work as a whole.

By the way, this is just one out of the several underwater scenes that we have to bring off in our underwater set, and it's not even the most complicated by far.

As soon as Percy III had been spruced up and inspected, he was kept handy at the underwater set so that we could knock off that scene of his. "Knock off" —the joke was on us!

First we needed a big fish for Nick to be trying to photograph. We had our hearts set on a thirty-six-inch grouper as the ideal subject, but we're also using the *real* eel in the sequence. Every time we show him, everything else has to be half-size to make him look twice as big. So we also needed an 18-inch grouper with markings identical to the large one we'd picked. Make that a few of each; it's always good to have a back-up. You can't be too careful.

So Teddy Tucker went fishing, but he couldn't find our groupers. Again he went out . . . and again . . . and again. No luck. We can't wait around forever, so we've decided to go with a 20-inch porgy. He doesn't have the star quality of our three-foot grouper, but he'll have to do. Neither does he have his doubles, but we'll worry about that later.

Working with even a smart animal is trial enough, but there's just no way to train a fish. Rather than trying to, we tranquilized our porgy so it would at least stay put for the scene. Percy was weighted, and filament was attached to his head and tail so that he could be pulled across the screen. We did a take. Percy rattled across like an old railroad car . . . not exactly the swift, sleek look we were going for. "Let's do it again, gentlemen," Yates intoned into his mask. The special effects divers got ready to pull Percy again. Just then the porgy came to and darted away. He was caught and Quinaldined again. Roll 'em! Now Percy was OK, but the porgy had too much Quinaldine in him and he was lolling on his side with a glazed look in his eye. Again! This continued for fifteen takes. Even the serene Peter Yates was exasperated. The upshot: We'll have to figure out a new way to get Percy across the screen, and our porgy has OD'd on Quinaldine.

August 20

So special effects man Ira Anderson went to work. He devised a new method of moving Percy via a counterbalanced pulley that literally catapults him across like a stone out of a slingshot. Ira then dreamt up a special little harness that invisibly attaches a dead fish to Nick's camera so that when Nick moves, the fish seems to glide before him. It's clever, but now we were back to looking for our fish again.

The other special effects stuff like the strobe flashing —the stuff we thought would be the hardest—went without a hitch. But the rest of the sequence dragged on and on. We ended up having to buy two fish from an aquarium in Florida *and* go through several more from Bermuda waters before completing the scene . . . nearly three months after we began it.

So much for knocking off the old Percy-grouper scene, and a lesson learned: there's really no such thing as simply knocking off a scene—any scene—in our underwater set. Every sequence is a battle, and every piece of usable footage shot, a triumph.

At the height of tourist season, virtually every bed available for visitors is already occupied by female tourists and their male companions. Of course, we could let it be known that we work on *The Deep,* which gets us a place—for a price. Many locals— especially those who deal in goods or services we need, in this case realtors—have visions of fame and fortune. They view everyone working on the film as millionaires and thus prime possible players of the rip-off game played in every popular summer resort. The rules go something like this: We've got it, you want it, you can't get it anywhere else, so this is what you have to pay for it. That translates to as much as $1,200 a month for a one-bedroom cottage! "Deepers" wanting to squeeze into the colorfully-named homes along the Bermuda roads, like "Beautiful Melody," "Night Lights," "Neptune's Perch," "Sea Palace," invariably end up having to pay "Through the Nose."

Though the hundred or so of us had begun our Bermuda sojourn somewhat centralized, we are now spread tip to tip over the island. This problem, combined with our having two units shooting all over the place and a vast amount of movement back and forth, means that the usual film production walkie-talkies just don't cut it for *The Deep.* So we've become CB freaks. Radios have been installed in all the main production vehicles and attached as portable units to the belts of key personnel. Everybody picked their own names and had a good time with them.

Our radios, though useful, are the downfall of any semblance of secrecy on the production. Anything that's decided, any move we make, the local government or media always seems to be ahead of us. Anyone within earshot can hear what's going on. Just as unnerving as the lack of secrecy is being an unwilling listener to a personal exchange between two members of the company over the CB, since we all tend to forget that everyone else on the production is privy to our not-so-private conversations.

CB or no CB, there is just no such thing as a secret on the island of Bermuda. The incestuous atmosphere of movie companies everywhere is well known; in Bermuda, though, the problem is compounded. The whole island, after all, has only 75,000 inhabitants, and most of them are interrelated in one way or another. So it's no surprise that Bermudian gossip always travels at the speed of sound—and, while *The Deep* is here, at the speed of light.

Since there were no cars for rent (Bermudian officials strictly limit the number of cars and drivers) we're largely dependent on local drivers, usually owners of their own cabs, to chauffeur us around the island. Well, our drivers are regular guys. They're friendly, efficient comedians and, like many Bermudians, blessed with endearing nicknames that make them sound like refugees from *Snow White and the Seven Dwarfs;* among them, Poly, Sparky, and a charming old character called Winky. But cruising along in company cars, discussing production company business, it's all too easy for an executive, star, or crew member to forget that part of the drivers' currency for the day's work are the confidential tidbits of gossip and information they invariably pick up while driving us around. Some drivers are even bold enough on many occasions to interrupt a heated discussion with their own advice!

We have two completely *separate* film units going almost continuously. While Peter Yates and our stars are working at the underwater set, a second unit is simultaneously following them up picking up shots on various land sequences that had been shot previously; the mobylette chase which ends in the kidnap of David and Gail by Cloche's men, for example. Yates and the stars would return to the land unit which would become the principal or first unit, and Stan Waterman and the Gorillas carry on as a second unit in the underwater set or at sea, doing pick-ups, inserts, whatever. "First unit" always refers to the unit at which the director of the film is working; "second unit," to any other unit working under the direction of an assistant director or stunt coordinator. Though both units have been busy every day, most of the action during the first month in Bermuda has taken place up at our underwater set.

Today the first unit finished up one of the most dramatic underwater sequences in *The Deep:* David's tumble into the grave of the *Grifon.* As envisioned by Tony Masters and written by Peter Benchley, the scene begins with David, along with Treece and Gail, siphoning up ampules from inside the wreck of the *Goliath* with the treasure dredge. David accidentally catches one of the many grenades lining the hold in his dredge tube, and it is sucked up, exploding in an adjacent chamber and touching off a harrowing underwater avalanche. The explosion forces David through a ten-foot floor of sand and rock that had sealed off the ancient Spanish galleon below for centuries.

The sequence was so complex that the key action had to be done in two separate segments and edited together—the "fall off" and "fall through" as we dubbed them. The "fall off"—the large rocks tumbling off the side of the ship into the deep—took the better part of two days for special effects man Ira Anderson and underwater set dresser Peter Grant to rig. Three major units of rocks were hydraulically controlled and timed to fall off at different intervals from the back of the set. The stunt worked so well that we decided to go ahead and do Nick's fall into the *Grifon* chamber that day as well.

August 24

Ira Anderson and his team spent weeks on the "fall through," rigging the floor with a series of interlacing pipes which would be pulled in sequence, releasing thousands of pounds of rock, sand, debris—and Nick Nolte in the process. Now prop man Peter Grant removed the safety rigging which had solidified the floor of the upper chamber. Chris Challis carefully worked out the lighting, which would have to change in mid-shot as light streamed into the darkened chamber. A full-hour session on the chalkboard above the set reviewed every position of camera and lighting and every signal that Yates would use to cue the special effects men's moves.

The fall-through was an especially dangerous stunt. The interior walls of the cave could collapse; Nick's diving hose could rupture; in fact, Nick himself could be badly hurt by the enormous amount of debris set in motion. But Nolte again insisted on doing the stunt himself.

Underwater doubles Jacki Kilbride and Howard Curtis were stationed nearby just in case anything should go wrong as Yates ordered action. The shells rumbled loudly as they began pouring off the sides of the chamber and onto Nick with greater force than anticipated, unexpectedly forcing him onto his knees near the back of the hole. Half the cave floor collapsed. Yates, figuring that something had gone wrong, signaled for a cut.

Within seconds after all three cameras had been turned off, the remainder of the floor gave way with a roar and Nick began to slip—for real—into the hole! Giddings, Waterman, and Nicklin quickly grabbed their cameras and started filming again, capturing a genuinely surprised Nick Nolte as he is sucked down into the *Grifon's* grave, only half-acting as his arms flailed frantically for some unseen brace. It was a riveting sight. We had to do it all over again. Again the rack of ammunition was rigged; again all the interlacing pipe and the hundreds of pounds of sand, coral, and debris were set.

It was a few days before the stunt was ready to be attempted again. This time, there could be no mistakes. Once again Peter Grant and the others removed the rigging which solidified the floor, Challis set up the lighting, Giddings carefully reviewed the team. Peter Grant took off a number of weights to make himself super-buoyant, and hung on the upper reaches of the chamber just out of camera sight, with ten ammunition shells in his arms. Yates gave the cue, the cameras started to whir, and with crack precision the rocks began to fall away obediently at the correct speed. The shells Grant now dropped fell before the camera, adding to the hail of ammunition from the rack at

Nick's side. Nick tumbled through the narrow crevice created by the cave-in and was completely gone from sight for several seconds. He suddenly reappeared in the lower chamber, hanging upside down by his air umbilical cord, fighting the flurry of water and sand all about him. Again on cue from Yates, two specially rigged giant water hoses were turned on full force, blowing debris, ampules and Nick toward the back of the cave entrance, creating the effect of water current rushing in to equalize the pressure in the newly revealed chamber.

It all worked perfectly! Our "fall through" is safely in the can, and Nick Nolte emerged without a scratch. Now we needed some cutaways of Jacqueline Bisset and Robert Shaw, looking on in horror as Nick disappears into the *Grifon* like Alice down the rabbit hole.

Besides mobylette riding, the big leisure hours sport for Deepers is, not surprisingly, romance. Love affairs on the tiny island flutter and die almost as quickly as the weather changes, which, in Bermuda, means every fifteen minutes. The more enterprising of the crew fly in talent from the mainland for special company on these balmy Bermuda nights. Some of the crew became notorious ladies' men, flying different girls here practically every week. Others wait for numerous cruise boats to dock and use "Deep" T-shirts as a magnet for their starry-eyed victims.

Our stars, of course, had their private lives too, and it was something I meticulously avoided treading on. One of the biggest headaches in motion picture making can be caused by a conflict between a star's private life and a screen relationship. In *The Deep,* of course, Bisset and Nolte have a very intense on-screen relationship, and their off-screen relationship is becoming close. Things were going so smoothly that we were more than a little uneasy when Jackie's boyfriend, Victor Drai, and Nick's girlfriend, Karen Ecklund, came to visit them. What was really strange was that Victor and Karen had met on the plane!

The four of them ended up sitting together at a

party given at my home for the entire cast and crew, and the whole mood was distinctly nervous for some of us, but they all seemed to have a good time.

Already one sizzling liaison had become a little too hot to handle. Right in the middle of production and right in the middle of his own important production duties, one key staffer departed immediately and without warning after allegedly catching his attractive wife in a compromising position with another member of the team. It was an unexpected storm, but George Justin, a seasoned veteran, weathered it expertly, keeping things in hand and quickly hustling up a very good replacement.

There's an axiom that goes, "They should give an Academy Award just for getting the film made." Until actual filming begins, every picture is touch and go, with the forces of the universe seemingly poised to bring it all to a screeching halt at any moment. But once a film begins shooting, it's like an avalanche: nothing can stop it. Movies have been made in the face of directors dying, team members slugging it out with each other, countries throwing on-location productions out, sets burning down, film being lost, stars not speaking to each other, costly special effects going haywire, and any combination of these and other disasters that the mind can conjure. Having weathered our all-too-typical *Peyton Place*-style crisis, it's only a matter of time before another pot boils over.

10
DEEP TROUBLE

∿∿∿∿∿∿∿∿∿∿∿∿∿∿∿∿∿∿∿∿∿∿∿∿∿∿∿∿∿∿∿∿∿∿∿∿

August 29

"The underwater set's rising . . . it's literally flying out of the water!" Benchley yelled on the phone last night. It was nearly midnight when this shocker came. Benchley and Tucker had been summoned from Teddy's home by the night security officer and had shot up to the B.U.S. to evaluate the trauma. Huge sections of the urethane siding that lined our underwater set were ripping away and catapulting to the surface! These enormous chunks of foam had so much buoyancy when they broke loose that their velocity to the surface was something like forty miles per hour, and they were tearing through guide wires six feet above the water line.

We raced to the set and surveyed the damage. The water level had dropped severely. It looked as if a giant series of blue icebergs were floating on the water's surface. It also looked like the beginning of the end for our Biggest Underwater Set. We'd already fought leaking pipes—which caused the water level to fluctuate and played havoc with our underwater lighting—and broken down sea pumps, for which we had to rush in a specialist from Boston with special parts. But this was the worst yet.

Nobody could really get a handle on just what was going on down there, not to mention how it would affect every other thing in this environment we'd built. Out set was a little ocean with mysteries all its own. Were any fish killed? Was all the water going to leak out now? Would the ecology of the system be radically altered? It surely looked that way. Tucker was clear on one thing: Anyone working in the set in the path of one of those urethane missiles would be killed instantly.

This morning we had an emergency meeting. Most anxious to know the exact prognosis for the B.U.S., Giddings slipped into the water and slid gingerly down its concave side to an open edge of the lining. He ran his fingers under another piece and *whammo!* Like a Poseidon missile, it shot to the surface and a scared gallery of fish darted back from its path. Giddings surfaced. "More will probably come off, but likely only in this one area," he told us. Amazingly, all the fish were all right, and the water level seemed to be holding steady.

Whether we can finish shooting this last week before our team ships off to Australia so we can drain and fix the set, neither Al nor anyone else can say for sure. The only thing we can do is to have the team lay a network of pipes and boards over the whole set's bottom, which will catch any pieces as they shoot loose . . . we hope.

Nobody else has been super-eager to climb back into the underwater set after that, but climb back they do. We have a movie to make here!

Although everyone's hesitant about going back underwater, Earl Maynard's fight scene is particularly strenuous and it's not the kind of work an actor looks forward to. Earl was not very fond of diving in BVI. But we'd been sure he'd get into it in Bermuda. He *had* to: he has a big scene to do in our B.U.S.—Ronald's climactic underwater fight with David. He probably would have been fine had we not plunged him in much too quickly in BVI, but now it's too late to begin again with lesson one. In dailies Earl has that same bug-eyed look of terror on his face, which would be funny if it weren't so depressing. And every time he's had to go back in, he's made a bigger and bigger fuss. Earl's from Barbados, and his speech is like machine-gun fire even when he's feeling pretty laid back: very fast and rhythmic and heavily accented and hard to understand. When Earl's feeling upset, his speech gets so frenetic he's *impossible* to understand—but then you've got all that sputtering and that angry look in his eye to let you know you don't want to be around to try.

So we were rapidly losing the nerve to keep ordering Earl into the set. One of these days he might just turn around and throw somebody's A.S.S. into the B.U.S., P.D.Q! Anyway, he's still much too stiff in the water to make a convincing heavy. We had to finish that fight scene, with or without Earl, and it began to look like it would have to be without.

The answer was under our noses the whole time. Peter Grant, our scuba-diving underwater set dresser, is well-built, totally expert and graceful in the water, and black. Though not quite as formidably structured as Earl, and blessed with a full Afro in contrast to Earl's balding pate, some padding and a bald cap did the trick. Peter Grant becomes a stunt double and Earl himself can be used for closeups. But Peter Grant also had a moustache that he had worked to the point of pride and perfection. If he was going to serve as Earl's stunt double, that luxuriant facial foliage would have to go, and that, he said, "would cost us dearly." George Justin was given the duty of negotiating with Grant for his new duties, and that moustache was one of the trickier bargaining points. He had us over a barrel, or rather, over a B.U.S., since we had no other possibility. But at last a deal has been fashioned.

Peter has worked so well as a stunt double for Maynard that even at close range you can't tell where one leaves off and the other begins. Grant's expertise in the water makes the fight really exciting to watch. A talented underwater prop man, Peter will be an unsung star of *The Deep*—he'll also be serving as a double for actor Dick Williams, our Slake, and as another anonymous villain as well.

Peter Benchley is here for a month-long visit to the set. We'd been plenty nervous about his arrival. A writer's presence is always a little awkward on a movie set, but Peter Benchley is the author of a script which has changed radically since he last saw it. But our fears were totally unfounded. Benchley's attitude toward *The Deep,* happily, continues to be as far from that of a literary prima donna as you could imagine. And Benchley is only too eager to pitch in when the occasion calls for it. He's already come up with all sorts of odd little suggestions and improvements. And ironically, after all our authors, Benchley was back to working on the script, especially on one key scene. The attack on Gail by Cloche's men (the "painted bird number," as the scene was affectionately called) had, through the various scripts, moved farther and farther afield of the original mysterious, voodoo-tinged encounter, and had lost quite a bit of its impact in the process. Benchley is managing to bring some of the scene's original flavor back into the script as it's now structured.

By now we've developed a working routine at our underwater set. Denny Breese and Pat McDermott, our delicate British hairdressing lady, huddle together above the set to relay Peter Yates' commands from below to the crew. Both Denny and Pat are needed for this operation—Pat to decipher Yates' English accent through the electronic distortion of the radio, and Denny to send the orders back down to the submerged crew by hydrophone.

The rest of the set bustles with activity, too. The cast has settled not so comfortably into their somewhat makeshift dressing rooms.

Under the large tent toward the rear of the set, the company gathers for breakfast and lunch. Lou Gosset always brings his backgammon board with him and recruits stray press people to play between bites. And Lou has plenty of likely candidates.

September 1

Not only are we busy trying to get our underwater filming done, but we're also trying to make the whole operation look good to an almost endless procession of press visitors. The key is to try to get the reporters to dive the set and actually view our underwater filming in progress; and the way to accomplish *that* is to assure them that it's easy and safe and fun. Hopefully, by giving them the chance to experience the process itself, the press would be in an ideal position to evaluate the difficulty and intricacy of our efforts. Out of sixty press visitors, we ended up getting all but two of them into our set. Not that it wasn't a big challenge for us as well as them; we couldn't very well expect a complimentary article if we accidentally drowned a reporter in our zeal to excite him about *The Deep*. And there were moments, even in our controlled underwater set, of real panic. It looked for a while like one journalist was not going to make it. He hyperventilated. His eyes bulged in fear. He forgot to equalize his air pressure. His mask filled with water. Giddings, using Yates' Desco mask, came right up to the new diver's face, took his arm and said, "Clear your mask!" A few seconds later, Denny relayed the message through the underwater speaker. The journalist looked startled. Al's lips weren't moving now and the voice came. Before, his lips moved and no sound! The neophyte peeled around; who was talking to him? In a state of total disorientation, he'd forgotten how to clear his mask. "Breathe!", Al's out-of-sync voice commanded worriedly. He had forgotten how to do that, too.

Lest it sound as if we were careless with our visitors' lives, remember that they were being taken care of by underwater notables like Al Giddings, Jacki Kilbride, and Peter Lake, who stayed right by their sides and made sure everything was disaster-proof. Eventually the reporter got the hang of it, and like others before and after him, passed with flying colors his complimentary course from what we were soon calling The Deep School of Diving. Diving really is unlike just about anything else, and after having been through it, every member of the press was not only impressed with what he or she saw going on in our set, but felt like they'd been through a real-life experience. And it's working; we get one great write-up after another. The funny thing is, it works almost too well; the contrast between all the complimentary press coverage and what really goes on behind the scenes is painful. We manage to present an attractive front, but privately, things are getting bleaker.

The underwater team is working with ever-increasing efficiency in the underwater set, seven days a week. But we're falling more and more behind schedule. There's just so much to do! And *everything* takes longer than we scheduled—in fact, everything just takes a long time, period. Even Yates' underwater commands, having to be routed through Denny Breese aboveboard, take maybe thirty seconds longer than they would on land. He often has to repeat them; or a team member has a question and pops up to the surface to discuss it for a few seconds. It may not sound like much, but the delays mount fast. The seconds turn to minutes, the minutes to hours, and before we know it, we're days behind.

We'd been worried since preproduction that Percy I and II wouldn't be ready when we needed them. Well, they finally arrived with as much fanfare as Percy III had before them—a few weeks late, but it doesn't matter any more. They were carefully assembled, checked out, repainted, and tested . . . and then put back into their wooden crates to wait for *us* to get to *them*. Our climactic eel scene is getting pushed back further and further. But so are several other difficult underwater scenes. Too much is being attempted in too little time, and it has become apparent that there's no way we're going to complete our main underwater filming before the scheduled Australia trip.

But we'll have to push back many key scenes until the return of the team from Australia—especially the final scene in which the eel bites off Cloche's head— and will consequently have to make major variations in the projected second stage of the underwater set's function. Originally, we were going to drain and then clear out and dismantle the entire set and put in a scale model of the entire ship, a miniature eel hole for work with the real moray, and a few key pieces at the bottom for pick-up shots. Instead, several key chambers now have to be preserved and stored somewhere in the set for further work, and other sets have to be restructured and repositioned. More nerve wracking—those extra weeks of work have to be squeezed into our already bloated schedule and budget.

All of the most technically difficult scenes on *The Deep*—including the land shots—are being left for the last weeks of our shooting schedule. The blowing up of Treece's lighthouse. The crash of the Orange Grove elevator. All these, on top of the key dialogue interior sequences yet to be done which, while not as technically difficult as our special effects, are the vital connective tissue of the story.

Having drifted ten days behind schedule and several thousands of dollars over budget, and considering a new twist—that the team will have to return to Bermuda to complete the many still-unfinished underwater scenes—we were asked to reevaluate the Australia segment. Could the shots we needed be done in Bermuda, after all? Needless to say, there have been some violent differences of opinion.

The studio wants badly for us to be able to do our shark sequence entirely in Bermuda, and there is truly nothing that Yates, Justin and myself would like better. But Giddings and Waterman, who had worked in Australia many times just don't feel the Bermuda waters provide the appropriate conditions.

Teddy Tucker, our local diving impresario, made the strongest plea for us to do the "shark bit" in Bermuda. In trying to help, he even went so far as to conjure an elaborate floating platform with sand on it to be hung from the bottom of the boat. It's such an absolutely mad, Rube Goldberg idea that we've absolutely decided to go with Waterman and Giddings' plan. Though Teddy is passionate and sincere in his belief that it can be done in Bermuda, we have to back the men we bet on. So it's definite: Australia is the next step.

Tensions are mounting. Two underwater staffers had to be cut from the Australia trip for budgetary reasons, creating disappointment and bitterness. Many of us have been losing our tempers and snapping at each other. An early joke in the production, that we'd better order our turkeys because we'd be spending Thanksgiving in Bermuda is suddenly too real to be funny.

September 15

But it's time to begin packing, a task that will take two days for the mass of equipment alone that has to be very carefully moved fourteen thousand miles to the other side of the earth.

Lunch during this last day of filming at the BUS—for several weeks, anyway—was a poignant affair. We felt as though the family were breaking up. There were promises to get together with some team members, like Jacki Kilbride, who aren't coming back to Bermuda. There were a few stray, mighty grim jokes about how some members of the underwater team may not be coming back, period. Still photographer, Keith Hamshere, took some group shots of the entire company. And Jackie Bisset skipped around the lunch area taking her own snapshots of the underwater team. She's sorry to see "her" underwater team go, for having finally mastered diving and actually learning to enjoy it, Jackie feels a real kinship with Al and the rest of the team.

Our dive team left for the Bermuda airport. And had a drug bust.

Not only is Romer Treece based on Bermudian lore. So is the *Goliath* wreck around which Peter Benchley wove the plot of *The Deep*. In fact, it was Teddy Tucker who first introduced Benchley to the wreck of the *Constellation,* a World War II vessel off the coast of Bermuda lying atop not one, but *two* other shipwrecks; an American steamer from the time of the Civil War, and an old Spanish galleon. Benchley knew nobody would believe that, so he cut the number of wrecks from three to two, which still raises a lot of readers' eyebrows even as they're wolfing down every page. But it's all true, even down to the thousands of ampules of opium, adrenalin, and morphine which the *Constellation* actually carries in its holds.

And it's all live stuff, too. When Benchley and Tucker told us about it, we wondered if maybe the Bermudian government should blow up the *Constellation* just as the characters in the story blow up the *Goliath* —to keep the drugs from falling into the wrong hands. "And kill the moray eel?" Teddy shot back. It turned out that Percy, too, was a real inspiration. When Benchley was concocting his piece, Teddy had tried half-heartedly to lure Peter to swim through the hole atop the boiler. No dice. Teddy hooked an enormous piece of shark to the end of a steel cable and lowered it over the protruding boiler. *Wham!* Out leaped an eight-foot moray tearing his meal whole hog from the hook. Enter Percy. So when Yates suggested writing Percy out of the cave and back into the wreck, it turned out that our own instincts were not only correct but accurate.

Anyway, the Bermudian government apparently figures they've got the *Constellation* problem under control because the ampules are nestled under huge bags of cement which the ship was also carrying when it went down—and which hardened into concrete when they hit the water. The ampules, as a result, are not usually brought up by sport divers. But our crackerjack underwater team had gone diving on the *Constellation* just for fun a few times, and they had gathered some souvenirs in the process! As the team filed through U.S. customs in Bermuda on departure, an unsuspecting inspector reached into a travel bag and rummaged through the contents.

Whoops! What's this? The agent brought out a three-inch glass ampule filled with a yellow liquid. OK, everybody, once more from the top. A close inspection revealed that almost every member of the crew had dozens of the little buggers, adding up to a grand total of over 500 ampules. But these people were not your average junkies. The ampules had been collected as souvenirs of their diving expertise. In spite of their having gone down thirty-four years ago, each ampule of the drug's concentrate was live and worth a small fortune.

It was only the fact that the ampules were spotted at the U.S. Customs headquarters in Bermuda that saved our team from real trouble. Had it been on the way to Australia, or back from Australia to the United States, lengthy explanations would have done no good. Luckily, local U.S. authorities are well aware of *The Deep*, the *Constellation,* and its background. A stern warning, confiscation, and some delay was the net result.

We've often wondered when the government would tire of the whole matter of the *Constellation*'s attraction, and someone would have to do something about that sunken pharmacy.

11

ONE IF BY LAND, TWO IF BY SEA

Our underwater team had barely left for Australia when some enterprising Bermudian reporter found out about the trip and decided he had the scoop of the century. That's how he wrote the story up, too. Huge newspaper headlines screamed that sharks were being filmed in Australia for *The Deep,* followed by a detailed "expose" with all sorts of implications about how the shark sequence would disastrously affect Bermuda's tourist industry.

Hoping to avoid exactly this reaction, we purposely hadn't broadcast our Australia filming plans around the island. But they hadn't been kept a secret, either, as the story implied. Director of Tourism Jim Williams is on our side. "That reporter has an overactive imagination," he assured me. "I should know . . . he used to work in the Department of Tourism." Still, the Bermuda government is in a tizzy. They can't really do anything about our Australia shoot, but what about all that remains to be done on this sunny little isle? It's theirs, and they might just "recommend" that we drop it from the film or else. Jim not only wrote an indignant letter to the newspaper's editor defending the production; he's also had to speak in our behalf before a special "shark" meeting in Parliament. The hubbub finally appears to be dying down.

With the underwater team gone, our underwater set has been drained and the fish let go. Reconstruction has begun on the site for the work that will have to be done in there when the team returns. The first unit has taken its boats and gone to sea, too. In fact, for these three weeks, the sun will never set on *The Deep*. Every minute of the day and night—somewhere in the world—we'll be on or under the sea.

The Deep has several key scenes that take place on the ocean's surface, mostly on Treece's boat, the *Corsair*. Much of the action is fairly straightforward: for example, dialogue among the three main characters as they head out to sea. But several scenes are fairly complex: Gail being attacked by and engaging in deadly battle with Slake; the villains cruising by and chumming up the sharks as Adam Coffin watches, and so on. On the sea, even simple filming becomes complex, and complex filming becomes nightmarishly so.

I can't stress the reality enough: you are totally at the mercy of the elements when you're filming at sea. The water plays havoc with everything from the company's stomachs—all but the sturdiest souls require seasickness prevention tablets—to the cameras. With that much movement, even your audience can get seasick watching the film. So a special rig is required to keep the camera steady and to compensate for the constant chop of the sea, and even with the rig, your subject is constantly bobbing in and out of frame.

Most ocean filming is done "boat to boat." A work boat carries equipment and crew; and a "character" boat—the boat that is featured in the film—carries cast, props, and whatever crew members absolutely have to be on board (the sound recorder, for example, to pick up the dialogue). During our preproduction phase, Director Franklin Schaffner, fresh from his own watery trials filming Hemingway's *Island in the Stream* in Hawaii, generously offered a pearl of wisdom earned the hard way. "Whatever you do," he told me, "*don't* film boat to boat!" Schaffner suggested building a special filming platform instead. But between the chaos of preproduction and the crunch of time, we never got around to taking his advice. And so here we are, filming boat to boat. But luckily Yates' experience on *Murphy's War* shooting at sea and the fact that Chris Challis is an experienced sailor really paid off. Also what Teddy Tucker doesn't know about anchoring and positioning boats is not worth knowing.

The surge of the ocean keeps changing the angle between the two boats, meaning, naturally, that nothing will cut together properly unless you wait for the sea to put you back to where it had you last time to complete a sequence. And the sun's movement across the sky continually changes the angle of light and shadow, so the boats constantly have to be moved around to follow the sun until, by late afternoon, though the sky may still be bright, you have to wrap or risk having footage that simply refuses to cut together.

All this is bad enough, but the worst thing about ocean filming is that old devil weather. With nothing around but sea and sky, you are vulnerable to its every whim. Wind? The water gets choppy, your equipment rolls around, everybody gets seasick, the boats bob up and down, you can't get your shots. Clouds? You get fluffy white formations in your sky where there were none the shot before, a glaring booboo that even the most apathetic film viewer will pick up on. If it's a day for night scene, clouds stick out like cotton clumps in a sea of black ink. Or clouds might mean you get rained on. Or any combination thereof, take your pick.

Weather is a constant factor in any outdoor filming, and in *The Deep,* of course, always a consideration. This month, though, it's become an obsession. We have plenty of cover sets—the interiors we work in when the weather isn't so hot. But foremost on our minds is getting that boat material out of the way. Here it is, September moving into October already, and even in balmy Bermuda that's autumn, which means fewer nice days and more wet, windy ones. We have to beat the change of weather before it beats us, in which case we'd face not only the wrath of the weather but the more terrifying wrath of Columbia Pictures, too.

September 18

Every film production uses a "call sheet," which tells cast and crew every evening what's happening the next day: where to meet, what scenes will be filmed, what equipment and props are necessary, and so on. Usually there's an exterior set, if that's what's needed, and perhaps an alternative—an interior if the weather's no good. Well, *The Deep*'s call sheet lists the following possibilities: a) if the weather's clear and water calm, the crew goes out to sea for boat to boat, day for night; b) if the water's calm enough to go out to sea but not clear enough for day for night, one of the key day scenes will be done out there; c) if it's clear but seas are rough, an exterior land scene; d) if it's wet and miserable, an interior land set!

Oh, it's cute, all right. But that isn't the end of it. The whole matter will get doubly complicated when the underwater team returns and the two units will shoot simultaneously. They'll have alternate calls as well, with weather dictating whether they shoot live in the sea or stay in the B.U.S.

On the bottom of the call sheets, there's usually a message from George Justin, who's in charge of assembling these monstrosities. His favorite is an exhortation to "shoot for greatness, for the Big Allagaroo" —an old school cheer of George's, which he intends as a cross between "for God and country" and "for the Big Gipper." The only consistently dicipherable message from day to day is "DECISION AT MANGROVE BAY 7:30 A.M." Which means, be at Mangrove Bay early A.M., turkeys, we're going to try to go out on the boat and we'd better not leave without you if you're supposed to be on it.

So we all descend on Mangrove Bay by bus or company car or mobylette and cluster around the little dock area, drinking coffee, eating doughnuts or bangers, and wondering what the weather's going to do. We turn to Teddy Tucker for our weather forecast. "Well, Teddy, is it gonna stay like this?" we ask if it's nice, and "Well, Teddy, is it gonna clear up?" if it's lousy. He's amazingly accurate.

Even the redoubtable Tucker makes a booboo occasionally, so there have been days when we wended our way through the rain back to the dockyard and set up on the soundstage that holds Treece's rooms— only to watch it become gorgeous an hour later. And other days, when we hung around at Mangrove Bay trying to brazen out the rain—and blew half the day waiting for it to clear up. But generally, our luck is surprisingly good, and even Tucker is amazed that the fickle weather is so cooperative for our first weeks of boat work. We've had two gorgeous weeks during which the one rainy day came on our day off . . . not much fun for the company, maybe, but terrific for the film.

September 26

One of the big headaches of preproduction had been our failure to cast several roles before filming began. The absence of an Adam Coffin in particular plagued us. The role is a key one. Coffin introduces much of the necessary background to the story, relays key information about Romer Treece, and drives the confrontation between Cloche and our heroes toward a climax. We knew early on that Eli Wallach would be terrific. Wallach is an "actor's actor," a veteran of both stage and film who's been in dozens of films, from *Lord Jim* to *The Misfits, The Good, the Bad, and the Ugly* to *Cinderella Liberty*.

Eli read the book, liked Coffin, and was interested, but there was a scheduling problem. Eli and his wife Anne Jackson, herself an actress of formidable skill and reputation, were working together in a New York play which would run into the summer. And since the Wallachs like working on stage together better than just about anything, we would have to work around that if we wanted Eli. We finally managed to work out an arrangement through which Wallach would take a six-week leave of absence from the play to be our Adam Coffin. That time limit would have to be strictly observed, so we promised to complete Wallach's scenes in six weeks, with stiff overage penalties written into the contract should we need him longer.

The Deep was blessed with the presence of two fine actors in two key roles. But in one crucial way, the parts of Treece and Coffin still remained uncast. We had to also find young actors to portray these men thirty-four years *earlier* in the opening scenes of the picture, set in 1943. In fact, one of these scenes, more than anything else in the film, establishes in a single stroke the relationship between the two men. Adam Coffin was on the *Goliath* when it went down with its cargo of drugs . . . a plot point now to be emphasized in the wreck of the ship which opens the film. The day after the storm, young Treece is walking along the beach with his dog when the animal starts sniffing and whining at a hatch cover washed up on the sand. Treece leans over curiously, opens the hatch cover— and jumps back startled. There's a man inside! He looks dead . . . and then his head moves slightly, his eyes blink, his mouth spews water. The man is Adam Coffin.

Luck is smiling on *The Deep*. Both actors have sons who bear striking resemblances to their fathers, *and* are the right age to reenact these early scenes! Robert Shaw's fourteen-year-old son Colin had to return to school in England before this scene could be scheduled, but with his father's permission, we've managed to woo him back to Bermuda for a few days to film it. And Eli Wallach's twenty-five-year-old son Peter agreed to play young Adam Coffin for us. The money he earned would be put to good use in the creation of his own animated films.

But our "discovery scene" as we call it, still lacks one thing as its scheduled filming date draws near: a dog. A well-trained, lovable-looking dog who would sniff and whine at that hatch cover on cue. Not so hard, you think? Well, as we've already learned, casting an animal is no less complicated than casting our human roles.

In the novel *The Deep*, Treece has a dog named Charlotte, and back during preproduction we expended enormous time and energy on casting this furry sidekick. While Yates and I sweated over the human roles, Peter Lake was assigned the task of finding Charlotte, or, as Lake put it, Deep Dog. She had to be long-haired and friendly, and, in addition to the usual tricks, she had to do things like lick faceplates and play wounded. She should also have a double, both as a back-up and to play young Treece's dog—her forebear of thirty-four years earlier. With other expenses piling up rapidly, we decided to try to avoid the cost of a professional Hollywood dog, and find a well-trained non-professional pooch. So just about the time we were launching our talent search for Gail, Peter Lake was launching one of his own, placing advertisements in newspapers and putting out the word at kennels for a dog "for a role in a major motion picture."

With bait like that, Lake fully expected to be bombarded with calls from starry-eyed pet owners. But as he notified Yates and me in a four page "bow-wow memo," the response was disappointing. Sunshine, a springer spaniel from Eagle Rock, was available and interested; so was a Monrovia dog colorfully named Hyper-Hank. And the owners of Nicky, a German shepherd in Industry, California, wrote to inform Peter that she could do everything from herding sheep and climbing ladders to balancing food on her nose. But, alas, just as none of those starlets had been our Gail, none of these animals was our Charlotte. Peter was soon spending all his time calling kennels, looking at puppy pictures, and writing nice letters back to the owners on the order of, "Bluebell is not right for us, but she sounds like a wonderful dog. Best wishes for her career." So we finally gave up and decided to pay for the dependability, reliability, and experience of a show biz dog. We hired a professional beast named Tiger, a Tiger double, and their young trainer.

Well, we've been paying, all right: to the tune of about $1,000 a week. With dog food and the trainer's salary and other tidbits added to that figure, each bark costs a small fortune.

But for all our investment, trying to film with Tiger was a joke, and on the water it was a total fiasco. If the trainer said come, the dog went. She barked when she wasn't supposed to, and clammed up when she was. This went on for one week. Every evening during rushes we'd hear the trainer muttering on the sound track: "Speak, Tiger, Speak. Speak, Speak, Speak, Speak!" Tiger was driving Yates nuts, and with the interesting triangular relationship developing between Treece, David and Gail, she was mostly an annoying distraction. So home all three went, special dog food and all. It meant scrapping some footage, reworking a few scenes, and editing out a continuous series of barks from the sound track, but it was worth it to have her out of our hair.

Distaste for the entire canine species was running at an all-time high on the production after that debacle, but we still had to find a dog for our discovery scene. So we dug up a local animal named Saucey. Saucey is not a professional animal by a long shot; probably the closest she's ever been to Hollywood is watching TV movies with her nine-year-old Bermudian mistress. The little girl advised us that she would perform as we hoped—but only if we put her favorite rubber tennis ball underneath the hatch cover along with young Peter Wallach. So that's what we did. And it worked! After all our headaches with our fancy, expertly trained Tiger, a chewed-up red ball elicited an award-winning performance from a Bermudian mutt.

Back on the water, work continues on our numerous ocean surface scenes. Boat filming is fun . . . for about the first half a day. Then it's an exercise in tedium. Besides all the purely technical difficulties of filming on the water, it's a grind; if you manage to avoid seasickness, it's exhausting both physically and psychologically; and even on a big boat, it's claustrophobic. Equipment and people are piled over every available inch of deck space.

But our cast is making the best of it. Jackie Bisset in particular is remarkable. Jackie's is the key role in our most difficult boat sequence: a violent struggle between Gail and Slake, Cloche's right hand man, which ends with Gail killing Slake in self-defense. For one key shot alone in the scene, Bisset had to be roughly thrown to the floor of the boat take after take

—seven times in all. It was grueling work, and Jackie deserved having lunch served to her and a quick nap. But Jackie invariably pitches in, setting up the lunches and bustling around the boat cleaning up after everybody else! Not exactly what you'd call a temperamental star routine.

As captain of our work boat, an immaculately beautiful white craft called *The Explorer,* Teddy Tucker is out there on the ocean with us every day. Teddy relishes the role of Ye Olde Salty Dog, which is OK with us since he performs it to perfection. In fact, Robert Shaw had prepared for his role as Treece back in Ireland with the help of tapes of Teddy's lilting Bermudian accent describing diving methods, anecdotes, and philosophies gleaned in twenty years of ocean exploration. He educates the crew: "Eat a piece of sponge. It'll expand in your stomach. Sure it'll make ya belch . . . but you won't be seasick!" He flirts shamelessly with the women on the crew: they're all as beautiful as Bisset herself. He enthralls us with accounts of his own experiences: "rapture of the deep," for example—that strange euphoria that overtakes divers as they descend past 200 feet deep or so, often with fatal results since the instinct for self-preservation completely disappears. (It's actually a physiological phenomenon technically known as nitrogen narcosis.) "I saw a beautiful blonde maiden in a lovely yellow dress," Teddy will begin. "She floated just a little before me, playing a silver flute, beckoning me on, always just a little further . . ." Teddy's delivery, matter of fact and yet magnetic, half inspires the hypnotized crew members to dive over the boat's side and find that beautiful blonde maiden for themselves.

Teddy's best friend and sidekick is another delightful, almost absurdly picturesque character named Banger. Banger was the model for Benchley's creation of Adam Coffin. He's thin as a rail, with skin like tanned leather, a wild, windblown mane of hair, and crinkly blue eyes that look like they've been gazing out on the oceans since time immemorial. He's also gregarious and funny, and Eli Wallach takes a special delight in hanging out with him as preparation for the role of Coffin. Wallach has already adopted Banger's accent, his manner of speaking, and even his walk; then topped off these perfect mannerisms with his own interpretation of Coffin's personality and private motivations for betraying his old friend Treece. He's cultivated a growth of white stubble, sports carefully applied stains in his teeth, and wears an outfit carefully aged by the wardrobe department to duplicate Banger's own ancient shirt and baggy shorts. Just a few days after Wallach's arrival, the transition from avuncular New York actor to Bermudian man of the sea is complete.

We're in luck. The weather continues to be good, so we've been out on the boat for days on end. But some members of the company are getting mighty restless. None of the actors playing the bad guys have much to do during ocean filming, and Lou Gossett has no boat scenes at all. He, like his henchmen, are all on standby, to be used on interior cover sets if the weather turns sour. They're getting paid for taking it easy, but the novelty has worn off quickly. They're restless to get to work.

Lou Gosset for one, did his best to keep busy and was nothing if not resourceful. Up there in his house overlooking the South Shore, he indulged his many interests and talents. He painted watercolors. He played the guitar. (Besides being an excellent actor, Lou's also an accomplished songwriter and musician.) He worked on a screenplay. He hopped around the island seeing some newly acquired Bermudian pals. But after weeks and weeks, Lou ran out of things to do. So he decided last night to hop up to New York for a few days, and flew off with our blessings.

September 30

Well, 7:30 this morning at Mangrove Bay didn't look too hot. Today we needed Lou. So George Justin called Lou in New York, where he was naturally still snoozing, since it was all of 6:30 in the morning there —and told him to get on a plane and come right back to Bermuda! Lou wasn't terribly pleased with this turn of events, but the show's the thing, so back he came.

You guessed it! . . . Lou's jet approached Bermuda through now azure blue skies and landed on a beautiful, clear, perfect afternoon.

Not all of us are quite as restless as Lou Gossett —at least, not yet. The first unit has been in Bermuda two months and some key staffers have been on the island for as long as five; but there are months more yet to come. We're still fairly fond of the place—we have to be—and *The Deep* has become part of the scenery.

Mostly the company keeps to itself, but relations with the Bermudians are for the most part cordial . . . Sometimes very cordial indeed. An attractive young local girl hired as wardrobe mistress is being squired around by a few of the film's young Turks. And one British-Bermudian romance warms the hearts of the crustiest onlookers. Bert Bowers, a widower on the English crew, met an attractive Bermudian widow, Julie Lewis, who was working as a receptionist in his hotel. A whirlwind courtship was followed by a wedding; and ultimately, the two will return to London to live upon completion of filming.

October 13

But the company's love affair with Bermuda and its people has been interrupted by some rather nasty incidents. Mobylette robberies are epidemic. We had our own Watergate break-in when production designer Tony Masters' harbor-view bungalow, called the Watergate, was burglarized one morning right after he left for work. The fact that the apartment was in a shambles and hundreds of dollars' worth of items were gone was bad enough. But the clincher was two knives that had been plunged into the bed mattress, as if part of some eerie voodoo rite. That really gave Tony and the rest of us the creeps.

The hilltop house rented by George Justin's assistant Sam Gellis, Sam's wife Alice, and production staffers Bill Rudin and Mike Nathanson, was the scene of yet another Bermuda pecadillo. Sam, unable to sleep, was downstairs in the den watching television around midnight. Bill and Mike had just left for a late evening beer. Alice was lying in bed upstairs in her room, absorbed in some magazine. A man with a knife crawled in through a back window and tiptoed up the front staircases.

The thief crawled up the last few steps and saw the open door to Mike's room down the hall. He slipped into the room and shut the door. Rifling through Mike's desk drawer, the intruder found Mike's pay and living allowance, better than five hundred dollars in cash. Still not satisfied, he moved out and down the hall into Alice's room. Alice, believing it to be Sam, didn't even look up until the door slammed shut. She turned to see a tall, muscular black man standing there with knife in hand. Immediately he was at her side, the knife at her throat. "Keep quiet. Where's the key to lock the door?"

"Oh, Christ, he's going to rape me," Alice thought. But she kept cool. She knew where the key was: already in the door lock, covered by one of her blouses hanging on the knob. But she didn't want to lock that door in the worst way. So she pointed to a few places around the room and shrugged innocently: no key. "OK—money," the man demanded. Alice rose slowly, no quick movements; the knife was near again. He looked her over closely as she moved across the bedroom toward the dresser. "Please let the money be there!" she prayed to herself.

As she slid open the second drawer and moved aside some shirts, a neat sheaf of bills fell into Alice's hand. She quickly placed it in his. Before he could react, Alice said, "There's more money downstairs."

"Who's downstairs?" the thief asked suspiciously.

"Just my husband."

"Let's go." He pushed her with the hand carrying his knife. Two-thirds of the way down the staircase, Alice bolted. She shot through the hall and into the den yelling, "Sam, help, there's a man here!" Grabbing a tennis racket—the only available weapon—Sam raced into the hall and began to duel on the stairs with the intruder. Then it hit him: "What's a nice boy like me doing, trying to be Errol Flynn in a situation like this?" Sam ran out through the den with Alice, and the two shot through several backyards and vegetable patches before finally finding refuge after pounding on a neighbor's door. They were safe, but a little poorer, a little wiser, and a lot more tense and wary about life on this "perfect" little island.

Tensions are mounting on the set, too. Peter Yates and Robert Shaw, working with the other actors, are continually changing the content of many scenes as they're shot from the script. Such changes are an inevitable occurrence in the making of a film. But often I get rather unhinged when I see them for the first time as dailies that have been already shot, since I'm the one to receive the brunt of Columbia's displeasure over such unannounced alterations. Occasionally the silence of rushes is punctuated with some sharp words between Yates and me. My secretary Missy, who is also serving as Yates' secretary during the filming, must feel pretty schizoid when Yates and I are having a disagreement as she types pointed memos back and forth between the two of us. Yates is often right.

Peter's methodical pace, his perfectionism and willingness to improvise, are certainly sterling qualities for a director, but it's easy to become paranoid when you have invested so much.

Even ninety days into filming, the art direction, production and construction departments are as harried as ever. Key sets for the production's final scenes are still not complete; several small but key roles remain uncast. The weather is growing more inconsistent, and after our first two weeks of unbroken boat to boat filming, we're having to come off the water every few days or so. We have plenty of cover set work to do, too, but the year isn't getting any younger, and it's nerve-wracking to have to extend our ocean filming schedule days deeper into October, when the weather could certainly do us in.

The Bermudian government set-up, unlike many American states and many countries, does not have one centralized film liaison department within its bureaucracy. That means we have to go to the individual department involved anytime we need a permit or license. Sometimes a single land scene, such as our lighthouse explosion, will require permits from as many as five departments, plus police and fire. If scheduling changes or the weather makes filming impossible, it's back to square one. But the government can be very helpful. Jim Williams has departed the Department of Tourism for a new government post, but his successor Colin Selley is very friendly toward *The Deep*, and even Jim himself keeps up a proprietary interest in the film. In fact, when he went before Parliament on our behalf, Jim had already left his Department of Tourism post. The locals, too, help out when they can. We have never been turned down on one request for a location, either private or public.

The Bermudians' helpfulness is no small blessing, but it can't alleviate the many problems of filming.

In my days as an executive, though involved in the making of films, I hadn't fully realized that there's *always* something to put an unexpected spin on the ball, no matter how simple a scene is at first thought to be. If it's not technical difficulties, then it's difficulties inherent in the script, or unhappiness on the part of an actor, or simply some little detail that's unforeseeable until you're actually shooting. What to do about Jackie Bisset's exposed breasts in the scene at Cloche's hideout, when she is forced to strip for Cloche? Though the camera will be trained on her bare back, Jackie is skittish about the frontal nudity the scene demands in the execution. Make-up man Eddie Henriques whips up two plaster concoctions to protect Jackie's modesty, which hairdresser Pat McDermott is then enlisted to apply. The scene had to convey sensuality to the audience, and Eddie's artful work went a long way toward accomplishing that. But, ouch! Taking that masterpiece off afterwards must have smarted.

October 14

The library scene in which David and Gail are directed toward Romer Treece by the librarian was another "simple" interior scene. Except for one slight problem: Just days before filming was scheduled, we didn't have the librarian cast. At least this gap turned out to be a blessing in disguise when Anne Jackson graciously agreed to do the role for us—partly because Eli had ended up in a cameo in her own last film and, as she cheerfully put it, she "owed him one." Anne, a small, pleasant-looking woman with a powerful presence, could hardly have set out to look less remarkable than she had to appear in *The Deep* decked out in gray wig, pink cashmere sweater and too-sturdy shoes. Yet somehow, in that get-up, with fewer than ten lines to speak, she played the part to cool perfection and absolutely stole the scene.

The next day, clear across the island, we hung Bob Tessier.

Bob, who plays Kevin in *The Deep,* is a powerfully built fellow, and certainly no stranger to violent death on screen. He's been "killed" twenty-one times; shot, hung, electrocuted, run over by a motorcycle, and even bitten by a lady vampire! Even with that impressive record, though, Tessier had never met his maker in quite the way he has to in *The Deep:* Kevin's body is discovered by Treece hung from the rafters, every limb twisted around, every joint broken grotesquely.

Ira Anderson and Charlie Spurgeon worked for days on a special series of pulleys and harnesses in which Bob could be strung up convincingly. And they had to practice it on him several times before they got it right. So just rehearsing the stunt took a fair amount of strength and stamina, and Bob got pretty red in the face from hanging upside down for minutes on end. Meanwhile, make-up man Eddie Henriques was in the back room working on some prosthetics—forearms, broken fingers—to be carefully placed on Bob to achieve the desired effect. Bob could hang for only a minute in the correct position, so when everything was ready, the scene had to be done very quickly. Robert Shaw did it all in one take. "Print!" Yates yelled.

It was only after we had done in Bob to our satisfaction that we progressed to the fight that caused his "execution." Though it was between two secondary characters and scheduled for just one day of filming, Yates was nonetheless determined to make the scene as powerful as possible. We asked for, and got, a stunt coordinator to come out and help block the scene. Bob and Earl threw themselves into choreographing the sequence with stunt coordinator Fred Stromsoe. They quickly came up with some nifty stuff, especially the idea of using an outboard motor, running in a barrel of water in Kevin's shack, as a weapon. So Ira Anderson quickly whipped up a specially altered outboard motor with rubber blades.

No dice! Tessier and Maynard were hellbent on using the real thing! And they couldn't be talked out of it. They went at the fight with a vengeance. As blocked out, Kevin has Ronald pinned against the wall at throat and crotch. Ronald throws a right cross, and Kevin releases his grip on Ronald's throat to block it. Ronald, with a vicious head butt, smashes Kevin through a closed door onto his back. Ronald charges in and is shoved back by a kick from the felled Kevin. Then he spies the running outboard motor in the barrel. He rips it out and charges its whirling blades at Kevin, who narrowly dodges the blade as it chews up the floor. Kevin now grabs the shaft and a nasty tug of war ensues, with the churning metal blade just inches from Kevin's face. With a final lunge, Kevin tears the motor free from Ronald's grasp. The fight rages on. In spite of Kevin's formidable strength, his opponent proves stronger. The ferocious Ronald breaks Kevin's neck—and as we later discover, twists every bone in his body—neck, arms, legs—backward at the joints.

Bob and Earl actually fought and struggled through every moment in this scene, and when it came time for the propeller bit, they did that for real, too, with the motor's whirling blades just inches from Tessier's face. Both actors were so involved in their parts that they stood in real danger of losing a few of their own. It was tremendously exciting to watch—almost too exciting.

The last few days have been rainy, so Jackie and Nick have spent them in bed . . . for our cameras, that is. The steamy weather meant that we had to begin on our torrid love scene between David and Gail weeks earlier than we'd originally planned, and Nick wasn't very happy about this turn of events. He was concerned that there wasn't adequate preparation for the scene. It's a key moment in the film. Not only do we want to quicken our audience's pulse; we really want to show the physical attraction between these two, solidifying their relationship with each other and with the audience. But the timing really was horrendous— Jackie's boyfriend Victor Drai is in Bermuda. While that's terrific for Jackie—she literally glows when Vic is around—Nick worried that there wasn't enough rapport between the two of them to do the scene right. But there was no choice, so the crew began setting up in Treece's bedroom while Jackie and Nick stole away to work on the scene for a few minutes alone.

October 15

Even with adequate preparation, filming a love scene is a tricky business. The actor and actress somehow have to forget that a bunch of grips and gaffers and lighting guys are standing around ogling them; and they have to get into the sensual frame of mind necessary to make such a scene really come across on screen. The camera's in close, the mood is subdued, and any wrong note will show up instantly. It's not an easy thing for any actor. And *our* hero and heroine—Nolte and Bisset—are both very private people. Our scene had special requirements, too, which made it a problem, not just in acting and concentration, but in choreography.

The scene was to begin with Gail lying in her bathrobe on top of David in bed as they discuss their relationship. Then at a key point, he opens her bathrobe and begins exploring, finally removing the top of the garment. Then, as if that isn't enough, David rolls out of the covers completely nude and onto the submissive Gail for the climax of the scene. Cut.

Sounds pretty simple—couples do it in the privacy of their own homes every night—but they don't have to worry about how it looks to a director peering at them through a viewfinder and a cinematographer asking them to please stay within camera frame. It was kind of like staging a bed-bound wrestling match. Nick, for one, attacked the chore with gusto. "OK, we'll put my leg here, then you grab me there . . ." There was no way to talk about it without sounding like we were blocking a porno movie.

Ask any lighting guy or assistant director if he's worked on a film where they had to shoot a love scene. He'll tell you in no uncertain terms, it's a drag. Claustrophobic. Clammy. Monotonous. Boring. Well, all that may be true, but it's also true that all those bored crew members somehow end up crowding around the set watching the action intently. Yates tried in vain to keep the bedroom set clear of voyeurs. But since it's part of the larger set of Treece's home, and affords plenty of views through open walls and staircase railings, he couldn't really close it off completely.

Part of the attraction, naturally, was the sight of La Bisset lying there in fetching near dishabille. Actually, though, it was Nick's turn to bare himself to the cameras. Since we figured Jackie had already revealed enough in two previous scenes—Gail's stripdown at Cloche's hideout and her attack by Cloche's men—it had been decided that Nick should do this scene completely naked. Nick agreed, but exhibited a funny blend of exhibitionism and shyness, fumbling for the sheets one moment, running around the set bare-assed the next.

Jackie was pretty blase about Nick's display, but a pretty local girl who vaguely resembles Jackie in auburn hair-coloring and slender, pneumatic figure, was hired as Bisset's stand-in, to sit—or in this case, lie—in her place while lighting is set up. The local is a sensitive, soft-spoken girl who embarrasses easily, as she did yesterday, when Nick decided he didn't want to get out of bed between takes so that his own stand-in, Kevin, could fill in. So the stand-in had to crawl onto the bed with a naked, though sheet-covered Nick, while lighting and camera guys set up the next shot. Nick pounced. He began kidding and hugging energetically, and she was embarrassed. "Stop it," she cried.

Finally she literally tore herself away from Nick and sat up at the edge of the bed with her back toward him, composing herself. Nick tried to woo her back. "Hey, hon, I'm sorry. I won't do it again. Come back over here, OK?" Well, that sounded like a sincere apology, so she turned around. And there's Nick lying there in bed under the sheet with a big grin on his face, and at a point about halfway down the bed there's this little tent . . . she got hysterical, and the crew howled with laughter. Nick had done it all with the script girl's pencil. But enough of the antics, Nick was finally ousted out of bed and replaced by stand-in Kevin for the duration of the afternoon.

But Nick didn't carry on that way with Jackie. In fact, the two were absolutely understated and relaxed as they worked the scene together, lying in each other's arms between takes, joking and talking softly, Nick calling her by a pet name, "Jackson." It was hard to tell where the acting left off and a real attraction between the two of them began. Especially today, when we filmed the scene's climax. The scene called for the two of them to talk . . . kiss . . . look at each other meaningfully . . . for Nick to roll over on top of Jackie . . . and kiss again . . .

"Cut!" yelled Peter Yates crisply.

Nick looked up, disappointed, and sighed.

Even though the weather is good, we have to come off the water and finish up Eli Wallach's scenes to avoid going into expensive overages on his contract. We have to do our dockside shark scene, the scene that introduces Coffin to David and Gail, and to the audience.

Coffin is working on the docks, weighing fish caught by tourists—in this case a huge shark—when Treece and David and Gail pull up in the *Corsair*. Treece calls Coffin over to the boat and shows him the ampule David and Gail have found. Coffin reluctantly confirms that it's from the *Goliath*. Still unaware of the *Goliath*'s secret, David and Gail demand to know what's going on, and it is Coffin who tells them about the thousands of other ampules still down there. Coffin considers the ampules of morphine his own long-lost possession, and is dazed by their sudden rediscovery. Summoned back by the Dockmaster to finish weighing the shark, he takes out the turmoil of his emotions on the tourists. "Weigh the shark yourself!" he cries, cutting the cord which holds the shark with one fell swoop, and leaving the creature to writhe and snap as it hits the ground.

Not only did we need our cast and several extras for this scene; we also needed a shark. And it should be a big one, the bigger the better. Naturally, we turned to our Bermudian water filming consultant. "Now you'll have your chance to get your shark!" George encouraged Teddy.

So Teddy and his gang started looking for a big, photogenic shark for our scene. He couldn't find us one. Night after night he went out. No luck. A shark, unlike other fish, must keep moving, passing water through his system to get oxygen. Instead of moving the shark, we'd have to move the water around him. So the production crew had designed a special holding box with a little water pump in it to keep a captured shark alive. But there was still no shark to put in it. "I'll find your shark!" Teddy growled whenever we asked. We began to get worried. In his fervor to find us a shark, he became like Captain Ahab looking for the great white whale. We let him keep looking, but we had to do the damn scene soon. So we finally broke down and *bought* a bull shark from a marine biologist at the University of Miami. It was eight feet long, a respectable size. There was only one problem: it was dead, and it would have to be shipped frozen. But by this time we were realizing that we'd have to make a few compromises.

So yesterday morning at the shoot, we turned up at Mangrove Bay to find out that Teddy had finally come through. Now we were up to our wazoo in sharks! Teddy had caught two six-foot tiger sharks and brought 'em back alive, and meanwhile our bull shark, courtesy of the University of Miami, was strung up on the deck. Should we use a live six-footer or a dead eight-footer?

By now the dead eight-footer has been thawed and

looks pretty sorry—its belly, which should be smooth and white, is mottled and red from broken capillaries. And since he's dead, we were not going to get much exciting thrashing around from him once he's cut loose. But we decided it was worth it to have a biggie, and so the tiger sharks were put out of the way and the scene was set up. Ira Anderson went to work, trying to get his jaws to snap shut on contact with the ground at least—something, *anything!* Teddy was still involved in the scene; he's doing a bit part as the Dockmaster. Banger was in there, too, so were a few members of the crew, and we'd recruited some real live tourists to play the proud shark-catchers.

We've been dying of curiosity about our Australian adventurers. Was our team getting the footage? Were they going crazy with ship fever? Was everybody still in one piece? The suspense was killing me. So I put in a call—right to the *Coralita*.

Amazing as it sounds, it is actually possible to place a phone call from Bermuda to a boat three hundred miles off the coast of Australia. You just have to be very patient. We had to hook up to the marine operator in San Francisco, and from there to Australia, and from there to the *Coralita*. Four hours later, we had our connection. It was exciting to hear the phone ring through on the deck of a boat thousands of miles away! Even the operator was thrilled. "This is the farthest, most difficult call I've ever placed," she said proudly.

The connection was unbelievable. It sounded like our team was across the street. And we were quickly brought up to date, although all the details won't be filled in till later . . . not at the amount of money that call cost! The weather is good, they're getting the shots, and everybody is still in one piece. Stan Berman hasn't even had to open his suture kit or break out the morphine. "We're behind you one hundred per cent guys. Keep up the good work!" I shouted into the phone. "OK," they shouted back.

And that, plus one other phone call, has been the extent of communication with our underwater team

during their Australian experience so far. We have sent
a few Telexes back and forth, too, and it was as wonderful as the phone calls when the machine started
pounding out the following wire message from Al Giddings today:

"ALL GOES WELL STOP WEATHER FINE STOP SUPER
SHARK MATERIAL IN CAN STOP EIGHTY PER CENT
COMPLETE STOP."

"ALL GOES WELL HERE TOO STOP GO FOR IT STOP"
we wire back.

And go for it they will.

12

THE DEEP DOWN UNDER

October 16

Our underwater team is back! As elated as the rest of us were at the news, our mood was equal parts anticipation and anxiety: glad to be seeing the Gorillas again, eager to see the footage they'd shot, and fully aware that the crucial final portion of our underwater filming is now staring us right in the face. No more procrastination.

The team arrived back in Bermuda tired, but with the air of triumphant warriors, their faces flushed with sun and the exhilaration of the experience. Yet when we press them for details of their incredible adventure, the team seems almost blase about the whole thing. Al Giddings has quickly resumed his matter-of-fact, we've-got-everything-under-control air. But there is something undeniably invigorating about tempting fate and living to tell about it, and even Al can't disguise his pride in having made the trip so successfully.

We've finally been treated to a recap.

By the time our Bermudian shark hubbub had been resolved, our team was well on their way, though just getting to their *take-off* point in Australia took three days. The Gorillas took off from Bermuda, changed planes in New York and went on to Los Angeles. Some team members live in California, so they took this opportunity to visit family and friends they hadn't seen since departing for the British Virgins months before. Then they regrouped in Los Angeles and boarded a jet bound for Australia, stopping along the way in Hawaii and Fiji.

In Sydney, the team was met by Guy Scott, the

young Australian representative of Columbia Pictures who was taking care of the team's transportation, hotel arrangements, and other miscellaneous tasks. The exhausted crew sacked out immediately.

The next morning our team took another plane to Rockhampton; then it was a bus through a landscape that evoked for many members "the American Midwest—thirty years ago" to a coastal fishing village called Yepoon. The village is starting to gain popularity as a resort, but it's basically a sleepy little place where people are most interested in their livelihood, namely, fish. Yepoon is a long, long way from Hollywood, California. Though friendly, the fishermen really thought it comical that a bunch of people were shlepping out into the ocean for days with tons of equipment to take pictures of sharks that would amount to maybe two minutes of a movie.

The boat Al and Stan had chartered for the voyage was the *Coralita,* an eighty-five-foot charter vessel owned by one Wally Mueller. Wally is an ex-shrimp fisherman and a knowledgeable old salt who doesn't really fit the part: not grizzly and acid-tongued, but chubby and amiable. When he's not chasing down poachers, Wally is escorting groups on the *Coralita* with his pretty wife Denise. It's a terrific boat, with complete facilities for sleeping and eating—and it's luxurious to boot: air conditioning, wall-to-wall carpeting, wet bar, cards, games, the works. And a good thing, too: our team would be out in the middle of nowhere on the *Coralita* for three weeks.

Now, that's a long time to be on a boat, a longer time than many of the team, in all their experience, had ever spent on the ocean at one time. So there was a lot of work to do on the Yepoon docks, unloading all the equipment, making sure everything was in tiptop shape, installing an air system, power supply, cables, everything the team would need on board. Finally all was in order, and toward evening of September 28, 1976, the *Coralita* pulled out of Yepoon Harbor, headed for Marion Reef in the Coral Sea 300 miles away . . . where the sharks were waiting for them.

Heading out toward the Coral Sea, our underwater

team didn't have it so good, at least not at first. When they set out from Yepoon Harbour, their all-night journey to the Great Barrier Reef was so rough that members were literally falling out of their beds. Some got so tired of continually climbing back into their bunks they just sacked out on the floor. Others managed to fall asleep in their beds with their elbows braced firmly against the sides to keep from tumbling out.

The next morning our team reached the inner edge of the huge coral reef, some parts of it taking the form of small islands that poke up above the ocean's surface. From there, it was still an all-day journey to their destination in the Coral Sea. Our team had dinner, watched the sunset from the boat's deck, and got settled in for the start of filming the next morning. They were by now 300 miles, or about thirty-six hours in traveling time, from the nearest land—all alone on a wide, wide sea.

The next morning Al assembled the crew around the *Coralita*'s rather cramped work space—only five by fifteen feet or so—and began breaking down the action of the scene. As now written, our shark scene was an entirely new amalgam of shark scenes from the novel, further reworked and elaborated in the script by Benchley himself and laid out in storyboard form by Yates and Masters. The concept of the scene was taken from an old western scenario, in which the hunting party has gone ahead of the wagon train. Returning, the group looks down upon the valley from their perch in the hills and sees a marauding band of Indians moving off in the distance between them and the wagon train. They have to get back to the wagon train without getting killed. In our case, the scouting party was Treece, David, and Gail; the wagon train was Romer Treece's boat; and the marauding Indians were the sharks. Our scene was to have all the tension of this classic situation, plus a few twists of its own.

David, Gail and Treece are in the lower chamber of the *Grifon;* David and Treece wearing full-faced Desco masks and breathing through air hoses wound through the ship and up to the boat deck above. What they don't know is that another boat has pulled up alongside the *Corsair*. Cloche, informed by our turncoat, Adam Coffin, of Treece's plans to double-cross him, has assigned his men to do a little creative chumming. They now fill plastic bags with beef entrails, blood, and fish parts and dump them into the water right over the *Goliath,* in which our three heroes are working. The great numbers of sharks thus lured to the area start attacking the bags, and our heroes' air hoses, and will likely gobble up anyone who tries to escape from the mess . . . all without a trace of the villain's handiwork. Treece and David are jerked around inside the ship as their hoses are attacked outside. They make it to the side of the *Goliath* and look up to see their path to safety blocked by marauding sharks.

Suddenly Treece is yanked out of the ship by a shark who has his hose, and dragged across the ocean floor until he grabs onto a loose piece of wreckage. David and Gail now hurry across the ocean floor toward Treece; pulling the dredge along with them. As Treece shouts instructions, the three quickly set up the dredge tube to spew sand and air bubbles up toward the surface, then cut the Desco hoses. Now all three must share Gail's air as they make a free ascent inside the whirlpool of air and sand, which protects them from the circling sharks just long enough to reach the diving platform of the boat and hoist themselves to safety.

Now, that's a scene more easily written than accomplished. Work on the scene had been begun live with the principals in the sea off BVI, and some wreck interior shots had been filmed in our Bermuda underwater set. More underwater set work on the scene remained to be done after the team returned from Australia, too. So not only did our team have to worry about getting film exposed and getting out alive, but also how all that hard-won footage would cut into the total sequence. Everything had to be planned as completely as possible before anyone went down. Al had discussed the scene in great detail with Yates before departing and now broke up the day's work into sections of the storyboard. We wanted, for example, shots of David, Treece, and Gail surfacing in the dredge whirlpool, surrounded by sharks; shots of Treece being dragged along the ocean floor by a shark who's running with his Desco line; sharks circling on the ocean floor, and so on.

Our stars had done an amazing amount of their own diving by now, but we wouldn't have dreamt of asking them to go to Australia and fool around with live sharks. There *are* limits. So the three key stunt divers who had worked in BVI before our stars began diving would now be reenacting the shark dredge scene in Australia for our cameras: Howard Curtis, Shaw's stunt double, playing Treece; Jacki Kilbride playing Gail; and Jack McKenney playing David. Of the three, only Jack had ever dived with sharks before.

Almost anyone who's been diving for years has had some type of encounter with a shark. But thirty sharks at once?! Actively seeking out the creatures by the dozen is something else entirely. To put it mildly, you'd better know what you're doing. Stan Waterman had been in these same waters during the making of *Blue Water, White Death,* and so had Peter Lake. And Al had been on the *Coralita* several times before, most recently during the making of *Shark's Treasure,* with Jack McKenney and some other team members.

The first time Al Giddings dove with sharks was in the making of a documentary called *The Predators,* and he had been literally sick with fear. Since then, he'd done it five more times, and by now this sort of thing was, if not exactly comfortable, at least fairly familiar to him. But it was anything but familiar to most members of our team. Al Giddings and Stan Waterman had the team's lives in their hands: they would be giving the orders, and everyone would be following them. And though they are the kind of men who keep their anxieties to themselves, Al later admitted that final responsibilty for his teammates' lives was very sobering indeed.

Most team members carried some protection

against the sharks, usually in the form of a "bang-stick"—actually a fast-load power head. This instrument triggers a shell which explodes in the shark, destroying his innards. But several members of the team, like the cameramen and the doubles, could not carry power heads. Even those who did have the weapons soon found them to be of limited value. A power head, like any other weapon, depends on human reflexes. And no matter how fast a human can move, rest assured that a shark who's set his sights on that human can move much faster.

The fact that our team members were usually all together in the shark-filled waters probably made them feel somewhat better about the whole thing. But if the truth be known, that wasn't really much help. Even in a close group of five or more divers, a shark zeroing in on one of them could strike so fast that no one would have time to do anything. The only thing that changes the situation by a bunch of people diving together, really, is the percentage: that is, with four other people around you, you've only got a one in five chance of being devoured. But no one was any more eager to see their team members hit than to be attacked themselves. But the bottom line had to be every team member for himself or herself. Each had to be responsible for his or her own safety.

Just in case the unspeakable happened, there was a surgeon on board the *Coralita*. His name was Stan Berman, and he was an amiable M.D. who'd also been along on the making of *Shark's Treasure* with Al. Stan was an avid scuba diver and excellent heart surgeon with experience in sophisticated operations. Hopefully he would not be called on to use his surgical talents, . . . but just in case he brought along a complete suture kit and a supply of morphine.

As the team prepared for their dives they doubled up as necessary on the many jobs to be done. With a pared-down crew and a lot to do, there were fewer clear divisions of duties; everyone had to pitch in as needed. For example, without the luxury of a wardrobe mistress and hairdresser, Jacki Kilbride and Jack

McKenney helped each other on with the wigs they had to wear as doubles. And everyone helped at one point or another with chumming up the sharks.

There were plenty of sharks around anyway, chum or no chum. They followed in the wake of the boat. They were hanging out in the waters below at any given time, twenty strong or more. Not surprisingly, nobody was ever falling all over himself trying to be the first to go in the water. But we didn't just want sharks cruising around languidly and ogling the cameras curiously. Our scene called for them to zip around madly in a feeding frenzy. And the only way to get them to do that was to chum up the water with big hunks of the dead fish caught by the team for just that purpose. But even that wasn't enough: all the dead fish in the world wouldn't get the sharks going. Sharks respond not just to the smell and look of food, but to the wave patterns caused by a fish in distress as it flounders about. So after chumming up the water, the team would have to spear one fish to get the action going. And when that dinner bell was rung for these none-too-discerning diners, it was very easy to understand why anyone would be wary about getting into those waters.

Spearing was mostly the duty of one man, Howard Hall, who works with Chuck Nicklin as a dive instructor at the Diving Locker, Chuck's store in San Diego. Howard was also around to watch out for everyone's safety. As it turned out, he had his hands full just looking out for himself.

One morning Howard aimed a spear gun at a fish and shot it, as he'd done several times before. Suddenly, the fish, instead of just floundering around obediently, began to swim straight for Howard—and so did about ten sharks in hot pursuit. Howard tried swimming away, to no avail. They were still closing in. He finally had to drop the spear gun and flee for his life. The sharks descended on the fish and demolished it in seconds. For dessert, they mangled the spear gun.

Not all of Howard's victims started for him, bringing their fierce natural predators in tow. But every time a fish was speared, the sharks would act the same way.

They'd lunge toward it and start tearing at it like a pack of wild dogs, and then, in a frenzy, they'd attack every other piece of chum in the area. That much you could count on—but little more. The truth is that sharks have very tiny brains. They've managed to survive from prehistoric times solely because of their speed and strength. Beyond their well-known instinctive ferocity, they're almost totally unpredictable. But the team knew that if anyone got hit by one of these animals, with two dozen other sharks around, a feeding frenzy would ensue in which our underwater team could easily become the featured entree.

In this uncontrollable environment, which changed by the moment, there was no telling exactly when, if ever, the specific shots our team wanted would materialize. For example, Peter Yates and Al Giddings had agreed on a shot of a shark running with a Desco line in his jaws. So, naturally, the Gorillas would go after that shot by placing chum on and near the Desco line and then spearing a fish nearby. But it didn't always work right. Sometimes the chum would show on the line—no good. Sometimes the shark would zoom up and grab the chum and zip away. Sometimes the shark would zoom right by the chum. Our team knew what they were after, and it wasn't exactly safe or practical to go up to the surface and discuss it; so it was a matter of doing it over and over again, chumming up and spearing, hoping to get the right shot. And the three cameras had to be going almost continuously, since no one knew just when, if ever, the stunt would happen right.

Chuck Nicklin soon discovered that the cameras came in handy for more than just filming. Because even after all the chum had been demolished by the sharks, they would continue to zip around restlessly, zeroing in on whatever they saw—including members of our underwater team. It was like being bombarded by dozens of live marine missiles. One time a shark made for Chuck so quickly and so directly on target that Chuck did the first thing he could think of instinctively—he hit the oncoming creature with his camera! The surprised shark darted away. Even without such quick thinking, sharks often bolted in fright from one of our Petermars when they saw their own reflections zipping right at them in its hemispherical glass lens—an optical advantage Al Giddings had unwittingly built into the systems months earlier!

Sometimes it would get so hairy that there was nothing for our Gorillas to do but just go hide someplace until the sharks calmed down and dispersed. The team would, if suspended in mid-ocean, make their way down to the ocean bottom—usually around eighty feet deep—and, if possible, find a "bommie" (the Australian nickname for the large underwater coral heads sprinkled around the reefs) to hide behind. The team tried to stick to the bottom as much as possible. Much of the scene's action takes place there, but also, as Denny Breese put it, "At least the ocean floor represented a hundred and eighty degrees where you knew no sharks would be coming from!"

But sticking to the bottom or hiding behind bommies was a luxury not everyone could afford. The doubles, Jack, Howard, and Jacki, had several shots where they had to rise up in the water encircled by sharks on all sides. And Jacki Kilbride had one especially frightening assignment; she was to rise up *alone* in the water for one key shot.

The fact that Jacki had on nothing more than the skimpy wet suit top and bikini bottom which Jacqueline Bisset had worn during the scene didn't help matters. Shark skin is smooth one way, but as brutally rough as sandpaper the other. Just one of the creatures rubbing past Jacki's bare skin would produce a nasty abrasion. The minute amount of blood thus released into the water would be picked up by the shark's incredibly sensitive olfactory system. Moments later, he would double back and head with lightning speed and accuracy toward its source, accompanied by any other sharks in the area—and that would all too easily be the end for our courageous Kilbride.

So here was Jacki, who had never dived with sharks before, rising up alone in shark-infested waters with bare arms and legs. That's guts, no matter how you look at it. Not that Jacki wasn't frightened. But Al had promised her it would be OK, and if he said it was OK, well, then, Jacki would grit her teeth and do it. She did . . . and made it to the surface in one piece.

Geri Murphy, the other woman on our underwater team, had an initiation that was every bit as frightening as Jacki's. Several members of the team were decompressing at about ten feet when Al gestured to Geri, a few dozen feet below, and then pointed to a spear gun lying on the ocean floor about seventy-five feet down. What he was saying, of course, was "please bring that up." Geri was happy to oblige, until she looked down. Dozens of sharks were circling around between her and the spear gun. Geri couldn't move. Some members of the team started laughing and nose-shouting through their masks, "Go on, Geri, go on!" But she was literally paralyzed with fear. So Stan Waterman left the decompression line, swam over to Geri, and hooked up on the "octopus" regulator leading to the double air tanks on her back. Together, they swam down and picked up the gun. The sharks circled around, but didn't bother them.

After that, Geri wasn't frightened any more—at least, not *as* frightened. The next morning she and team member Wulf Koehler were down in the ocean early, snapping pictures of sharks, having a high old time.

Other members of the team, too, had a similar trial by fire to endure before they could work in the shark-infested waters . . . like Shaw's double, Howard Curtis. Howard is no sissy. He's done just about everything in his time as a stunt man; he's been set on fire, jumped off cliffs, crashed cars, the works. But never had Howard Curtis gone diving with a bunch of sharks, and he was, naturally, a bit wary. One day was really bad. The sharks were zipping around like crazy and it didn't take long for one to come at Howard like a bullet. Unlike Chuck Nicklin, Curtis didn't have a camera to use in self-defense. He had no weapon but his wits. As the shark closed in, Howard instinctively kicked, pummeled, fought back! *And the shark rico-*

cheted away. After that, Howard felt somewhat better about the whole thing; his attitude toward the creatures relaxed into something he described as "healthy respect."

But they could never let their guard down completely. There was the danger of becoming *too* blasé. One morning Howard went down early—alone—to snap some pictures while the rest of the team was still preparing on board. Curtis noticed two sharks a short distance away, but didn't pay any attention; they seemed to be more or less minding their own business. After five minutes had passed, Howard had completely forgotten about the sharks as he happily snapped away. All of a sudden one of the sharks came whipping over him from the rear just inches above his head. Only the air bubbles rising from Howard's mouthpiece had diverted the shark those precious inches away. Howard was pretty shaken up, and after that little incident his respect for the animals was healthier than ever.

There were countless near-misses like that. The team was always six feet or five seconds away from a harrowing collision with a shark. One zoomed in on Stan Waterman and tried to take a bite out of his air tank. Another one came at Jack McKenney so fast that he literally had to jump up in the water to avoid being clobbered right in the stomach. The shark zipped right through Jack's legs and sped on. Day after day, everyone's adrenalin would get going at fever pitch. When the team came up to the surface between shots or to reload the cameras there'd be continual excited chatter "Did you see that!" "They came so close that time!" "He missed me by just that much!"

With that much excitement, there wasn't too much time for boredom or claustrophobia, even after weeks aboard the *Coralita*. The team was too exhausted, the work too demanding, for restlessness to settle in. And the experiences they were experiencing together every day created an intense camaraderie that bypassed the tensions which would certainly explode in almost any other group of people living so close for weeks on end.

Wally's wife, Denise, cooked the meals, and she was, happily, a wizard at stretching the food supply while managing to make everything taste terrific. After dinner, there were books to read, conversations about the day's activities. Maybe a poker game would take shape. Al Giddings is as aggressive and intent a player as he is a diver, and he took those games very seriously, especially since they were played for money.

There really just wasn't much time for shenanigans. The team was working eight hours a day with the briefest of lunch breaks, seven days a week, since the trip was costing too much for them *not* to. Besides, what else is there to do when you're 300 miles off the coast of Australia? The group soon discovered that they had to move around periodically to different areas within the reef. Not because of the weather: After an initially rough few days, the Pacific was calm as glass, with 100 to 200 feet visibility the whole time our team was out there. But the sharks, after their hunger had been satisfied in the first frenzies of feeding, began to move slowly and warily, as if, now that their bellies were full, they had time to size the situation up carefully before deciding whether to stick around. They were a lot less frightening at those times, but also a lot less photogenic as they drifted languorously through the waters. So our team would move on in pursuit of new sharks, as hungry and mean and hairy as these guys had been just a few days before. They ended up moving and filming in three different locations within the huge coral rock formation called the Great Barrier Reef: Marion, Lihau, and Diamond Island.

And so it went . . . to an ultimately safe and successful conclusion.

13
THE BIG BITE

As it turned out, it wasn't the last of *The Deep*'s shark adventures. Of the 24,000 feet of film—over four and a half hours' worth—that the team had shot in Australia, most was right on target. And some— that of Howard Curtis peeling off the marauding sharks —was sensational. But we still needed close-ups of sharks gliding in front of the camera with our stars clearly in the frame to really cinch the scene. So we decided to get those pick-ups . . . in our underwater set. Certainly trying to stage them in the open sea would be a total fiasco.

Finding a large shark had been no easy task for Teddy Tucker when we needed one for our Mangrove Bay dock scene, and it wasn't easy now, especially since it was imperative that it be fresh—in other words, alive. Finally, the persistent Teddy found us a six-foot-plus shark to work with. We had no intention of fooling around with a live shark for close-ups. So we held our sharks in Teddy's ocean pen and on "S" Day, today, gave John Hart the word: Kill 'em and bring 'em up to the B.U.S.

Hart, in a six-foot rowboat, with an assistant at the oars, first had to lasso our sharks. When he finally got the noose around the creature's head, the oars had outlived their usefulness. The boat caromed around at full wake in tow of the angry shark. John almost went overboard—and this was no time to be falling in! Finally the two men hauled the thrashing animal out of the ocean and administered an overdose of Quinaldine until it died, then trucked it up to the underwater set. The idea was to push the dead shark before the cameras with our stars in the shot so that, in a quick cut, it would look as if it were zipping past and through our threesome in a feeding frenzy.

October 24

After the sharks were unloaded at the B.U.S., Eddie Henriques had to do a make-up job on one of them, patching its nose and the top of its head where it had bruised itself banging into the shark pen. The set was full of curious onlookers as the shot was set up. Production Designer Tony Masters, not exactly the world's biggest diving enthusiast, had donned a wetsuit that day and was working in the back of the set on the *Goliath* model. Chuck Nicklin, with some help from Henriques, took the shark from the makeup table and put him in the water near the inflow gate so he wouldn't dehydrate. The team was assembling in one of the camera shacks for a brief skull session a few minutes later when a scream and a splash, in that order, rang out across the set. Tony Masters, in his full-length fire-engine-red wetsuit had catapulted himself out of the back part of the underwater set with a screech and was hanging onto the metal tubing just above water level. "There's a shark in here!" he cried.

"Yeah, Tony, we know. It's dead," laughed Nicklin.

"Bullshit!" Tony hollered. "It just came roaring by me!"

Apparently nobody had told our sharks they were supposed to be dead, and sure enough, the amazing qualities of this strange creature had allowed it to snap back. This was no joke. Giddings and Nicklin knew all too well that the animal could now be dangerous as hell. As for me, I figured, "Why not have a peek?" Then, if anyone asked if I was in the water when the live shark scenes were done, I could brag, "Of course!"

The animal acted like a member of the Screen Actors Guild as work on the necessary shots began. It bit the hose, raced at the camera, and charged the bags of chum, giving us every opportunity to get great footage. All was going well as I watched, so up I went to report to all the fascinated landlubbers hovering around topside that there was "nothing to be afraid of, guys!" Ten or fifteen cast, crew, and locals were standing around the entry platforms as I babbled on. Chuck Nicklin surfaced next to me and joined the conversation. Suddenly Nicklin pulled the shark right out of the water with his hand and the creature surfaced thirty inches from me! The animal's jaws were agape, and its eyes were right on me. I must have had a hundred and twenty pounds of equipment on, but with a scream I made Tony's earlier exit look like slow motion. Later that afternoon, Yates finally got the scene on film—no thanks to my courageous coverage!

It's nice having what was probably our single most expensive and dangerous underwater scene in the can at last, but the light at the end of the proverbial tunnel is still nowhere to be seen. On land, on the ocean surface, and in our underwater set, we still have all too much to do. I never would have believed that four months into production, we'd still be casting, building sets, and storyboarding, but that's just what's happening. And Columbia is rightly all over us to finish up *fast*.

The storyboards posted at the underwater set now reflect the huge amount of work yet to be done within its confines. So does the set itself. One month ago, our B.U.S. was the home of a series of interlocking chambers centered in its own small ocean: our *Goliath*. Now the B.U.S. is a bewildering hodgepodge of variously proportioned sets coexisting side by side like unacquainted neighbors. At the far end of the set, a twenty-five-foot high cliff and an eight-foot sunken model of the *Goliath* resting perilously close to its edge were built to bring an element of the script to life. Our ship was to be sent into the deep when Treece, consumed with anger over Kevin's death, decides to blow it and all its drugs out of Cloche's reach forever. Months of design and construction work in our fiberglass and scenic departments went into creating a submerged *Goliath* that combined elements of the actual *Rhone* in the waters of BVI with the *Goliath* set designs conceived by Masters and Maxstead for use in our opening scenes.

Just a short distance away is a huge piece of white plastic sheeting stretched against one whole side of the B.U.S., against which we'll photograph our actors swimming by. A special optical process called a "matte" will be used to reduce these figures and overlap them against fixed-camera shots of the *Goliath* model, to create the panoramic views we need of divers swimming across the entire wreck, and to firmly establish the wreck's geography in the audience's mind.

The B.U.S.'s shallow end, once used for press diving lessons, now features an intricate set for housing and filming our real seven-foot eel in his own half-size eel set. On the other side of the huge white screen, the full-sized eel chamber lays in spooky darkness almost directly beneath the surface work gangplank, awaiting its occupant: our full-sized mechanical eel, Percy.

October 28

The final confrontation between Treece, Cloche and Percy can be put off no longer, and it's one we all dread. Even before Percy's entrance, the scene will be an extremely difficult one. Treece is down at the wreck laying explosives to blow the ship up when Cloche swims down and over the ledge and shoots a spear into his flank. Then, drawing Treece in like a fish, he prepares to kill him with his knife. Treece knows he can't chance the drugs falling into Cloche's hands now, and struggling valiantly against the villain, he pulls the fuse igniter. In three short minutes—no matter who wins—the whole mess will blow. The two engage in furious battle, growing entangled in the spear gun cord as they struggle, literally locked together in a death grip. Treece sees the eel hole nearby, and in one burst of power tries to maneuver Cloche toward it and his head into the hole. Then Cloche unwittingly spins around and twists Treece into the same position. Now Treece himself is right in the eel's path! With a final burst of strength Treece twists Cloche around toward the hole again. The eel strikes! Cloche is looking directly into the hole and his expression turns to one of sheer horror as the moray's jaws close down on his head. His flailing arms yank Treece's mouthpiece out as he is dragged, still hooked to Treece, into the eel's lair. Cloche's arms and legs twitch spasmodically as the unseen eel crushes his head. Treece, still unable to untangle himself and get his air supply is fast fading and looks doomed until David risks his own life to come to his rescue.

Just trying to stage this fight in our narrow underwater chamber will be unbelievably difficult, not to even mention the problem we had of making sure the audience could tell what was going on in the darkness, bubbles and confusion. But the final ten seconds are the worst of all. The eel attack will have to be built out of an entire series of shots on two different sets (the miniature and full-sized eel holes); featuring three "Percys" (the real seven-foot eel, and our two mechanical eels, one with soft teeth, one with hard), and *four* "Cloches" (Lou Gosset, his stunt double Richard Washington, the "munchkin" of Gosset, and the "squish head"—the head of Gosset which will be caught in the final steel-toothed bite)!

An excellent local seamstress has made complete little outfits for the mini-men, down to cute little sneakers for the half-sized Treece. And Eddie Henriques has done a terrific job on making up the munchkins. He had to experiment with all sorts of mediums before coming up with some oil-based makeup which would not only look real but would resist the damaging effects of salt water.

But no matter how authentic the munchkins look to the eye, they can only be shown briefly on the screen with the live seven-foot eel. We can, to some degree, count on audience attention being riveted toward the eel in these shots, but we still have to plan them very carefully, both to keep the models from looking phony and to make sure they cut in with shots of the real Shaw and Gosset. So just what's the best way to use the real moray? Back during preproduction, our plan had been to sedate the eel with Quinaldine and suture the head of Cloche with monofilament thread into his mouth. We would then fit these, with the half-sized Shaw, into position in the half-sized set. When the eel came to, he would start thrashing around trying to get this thing out of his mouth, and to a viewer, it would hopefully look like an attack on Cloche.

But what if it doesn't? We really want some footage of the eel biting down on the model's head and drawing it into the hole, which, with this method, we won't get. So we've begun playing with other ideas, too. It's become a company contest: Choreograph *The Deep*'s "Big Bite"!

One possibility was to kill an eel and control its movement with a flexible metal rod inserted through the rear along the length of its body and into the mouth, skewering the head of the Cloche mini-man shish-kebab style. Teddy Tucker caught a four-foot speckled eel and we tried this approach out, with Peter Grant performing the actual eelicide. And it looked like it just might work. But now there were outraged cries from the company. *The Deep* has spontaneously formed what could be called the SPCE (Society for the Prevention of Cruelty to Eels). Everyone grew very teary at the thought that a vicious moray which would as soon take a limb as take a look at them was being killed for the movie. Not even that might have stopped us, but the seven-foot eel we were working with technically belonged to Bermuda, and we'll have to find another eel to skewer if we are hellbent on using this technique. However, we can't find any more eels of the right size and color.

November 1

Finally, in desperation, we put in a call to Kym Murphy, our marine biologist, who had long since returned to his home and job in San Diego, California, and begged him to find us an eel. We have had casting calls for actors, actresses, divers, dogs, sharks, wrecks—and now, eels! Kym, after a full week of anxiety, came through with an eight-foot moray. Elated, we eagerly awaited its arrival. Two days later, the New York authorities called to tell us our eight-footer had been fed before shipment and had choked to death in its too-small container.

We turned again to Teddy. From the Bermuda waters he disgorged a prize moray with whom all our live key shots will be made. The skewer technique will never be used, and our new recruit will safely be returned at shoot's end to its own reefy shoals. That happy homecoming will have to take place later, though. For now, our real live eel is still badly needed.

In the meantime, there's been a brainstorm: get the moray to go for Cloche's head *voluntarily*. He'll do it quickly enough if it smells like dinner. So we've opened the Cloche munchkin's head up, filled it with fish, and closed it again, confident that it will prove an irresistible treat to our moray.

Meanwhile, the moray is oblivious to our plans for him. In fact, he's oblivious to everything. His set had been constructed so that he could be trapped inside his hole without light or food until filming began. These weren't the most pleasant accommodations for our guest star, but our reasoning was that when we opened the trap door and let him out, he would be angry, restless, and hungry, and would lunge out of there just like we wanted him to. The set itself, unlike the holding lair, is enclosed on two sides by glass so that lights can be stationed on the other side and we can film the eel coming right toward camera. There's no escape for the creature, so we can use him again and again if necessary.

As had happened to us countless times before, the reality of filming had little sympathy with our best-laid plans.

We had never considered the possibility that our poor eel would react to his release from the dark chamber in a way that was anything but energetic. When everything was ready—prop man Peter Grant holding the munchkin carefully in place from just out of camera range, Petermars whirring, lights lit—the trap door was raised . . . on nothing. Seconds passed. Where the hell was the eel? Finally the long, green, sinuous creature—our boy—stuck his head out looking as dazed as Rumpelstiltskin waking up from his centuries-long nap.

The Cloche model's head was right under the eel's nose, and he dutifully gave it a sniff. But he wasn't terribly interested in the munchkin. He lazily, dazedly drifted his huge body past its head after a moment and right toward Peter Grant. Our prop man suddenly found himself literally nose to nose with a seven-foot moray. Grant kept cool, gently waving his hand under the eel's undulating torso, trying to shoo him away and toward the mini-Cloche's head. *"Cut!"* called Peter Yates as the moray drifted around the set in confusion.

The eel was herded carefully back into his hole, the shot set up, and the trap door opened—again and again. And every time, the eel ignored the fish-filled rubber head in favor of a meaningful beady-eyed encounter with Peter Grant. Our moray eel was in love! "He's tired," John Hart told us. Hart was the young marine biologist who'd replaced Kym Murphy when Kym had to return to California months earlier. John was good at his work, but he'd never been on a motion picture before, and the exigencies of film production just weren't as familiar to him as the intricacies of marine life. "The eel's overworked," John insisted. "He needs a rest."

Robert Shaw, Jacqueline Bisset, and Nick Nolte are working their asses off underwater, and we've got a moray eel who's a prima donna? It figures! Today we saw the dailies of our live seven-footer from five days before, and they were excruciating to watch. Tony Masters and Eddie Lima talked the problem over in frustration as the eel, up there on screen, did everything but what he was supposed to do. All he had to do was lunge out of his hole, open his jaws, and close them on Cloche's half-size head—it was so simple! Why, even a hand puppet could do it.

Tony and Eddie looked at each other. A hand puppet . . . ? And yet another method for completing our eel attack was born. A hand puppet! But not like something found on Shari Lewis or Sesame Street. This baby will have to be very cleverly designed if it's to look authentic. It's worth trying—at this point everything is worth trying—but there's not much time.

Eddie Lima quickly got to work on a sculpture which would provide the mold for a perfect replica of our eel, to be worn and operated by underwater propman Peter Grant. Meanwhile, marine biologist John Hart has been rewarded for his solicitous attitude toward the weary eel with a nasty rip out of his arm when he tried to capture the creature and remove him from the set.

The eel wasn't the only one who's tired. The whole production is beginning to take on the mood of something that's just gone on too long. And just like the eel, we're beginning to snap at each other to vent our weariness and frustration. We're now two weeks behind schedule, and Columbia had laid down a strict finishing date. We'd have liked nothing better than to finish by then, but it just doesn't seem possible. Still, we have to try, and the production has become frantic as everyone steps up their pace. Our stars are now zipped around to as many as three locations in one day. Nick will ride a mobylette for a key pick-up in the morning on one side of the island, dive in the B.U.S. at lunch, and do a boat dockside scene in the afternoon. The call sheet has reached new heights of complexity: between work at the underwater set, land unit work, various inserts and pick-ups, we now have filming alternatives that go from A to *H!*

Our Orange Grove elevator scene, originally scheduled for two days, ended up being filmed over a *three month* period of both first and second unit work before it was completed today.

David and Treece are returning from their night dive together when David sees that the Orange Grove cottage lights are out. Gail may be in danger! He races across the beach toward the elevator. But the cage is at the top of the shaft—and an ominous figure, Cloche's henchman Wiley, is watching from above. Suddenly two more baddies emerge, seemingly out of nowhere, and block David's path. The elevator starts and the counterweight begins to rise. David escapes his pursuers, jumps onto the counterweight and rides it up. Wiley, in the descending car, intercepts him and they struggle furiously. The motor starts to burn as the weights come loose from the counterweight. David pulls free of Wiley and shoves him deeper into the cage as he begins to climb up. Suddenly the last weights fall from the counterweight and the elevator cage breaks loose. Wiley screams in horror as he is carried to his death in the plummeting cage, which crashes to the beach over a hundred feet below seconds later. The lashing cable hurtles past David and knocks him off his perch on the flimsy shaft and down several feet before he can catch hold of the superstructure again at the last possible instant. Hand over hand, he now struggles up the remaining distance to the top.

Just about the only blessing of this difficult sequence is that it took place on land instead of underwater. Still, it was one challenge after another. There was no way we could light up the whole cliff, so Chris Challis had to figure out how to do day for night in a location where everything was glaring white: cliff, sand, sky. Our special effects team had to figure out how to crash the elevator from 120 feet high without really crashing it, but we ended up having to do it for real anyway, because there's nothing like the real thing. And the scene, besides being technically difficult, was dangerous. Bob Minor, the actor playing Wiley, was also a professional stunt man, but Nick Nolte was not. The sequence was complex enough to require the services of a "gag" man—a film stunt coordinator whose job it is to work out the choreography of the action. A gag man's services were especially needed to help orchestrate the climax of the scene, when the elevator was to drop away, the counterweights crashing to the cement pad below and knocking David off his perch a few feet before he can make his final lunge.

So the second unit, under the direction of an excellent gag man named Max Kleven, of *Rollerball* fame, laid the groundwork of the scene with some long shots of a stunt double for Nick. The stunt double was available for some first unit work too, but now Nolte insisted on getting up there to tussle with Bob Minor himself. To prevent Nick being knocked off his precarious elevator perch for real, the scene had to be done with great care. And Director Peter Yates, who had to capture all this on film, was in a very precarious position himself as he directed the sequence from a large makeshift basket suspended on steel wire from the tip of an enormous crane. Yates was swung out over the ledge and lowered down about seventy-five feet to a point facing the elevator cage, so that he could capture Nick at his most perilous moment. It was a test of nerves for both Yates and Nolte, and if the final cut scene is half as harrowing as the filming of it was, we'll be in good shape.

The tensions of filming have moved off the set, too. The English land unit was expected to finish up before the underwater team, and they've been given their two-week notices, an absolute requirement. But what two-week notices! They're about as easy to decipher as the call sheet. "You are hereby given two-week notice as of this date: however, we reserve the right to rescind this notice in the next seven days, and at the end of fourteen days, if it becomes necessary, we hope and trust you will be available for work for an unspecified additional number of days . . ."

That's confusing enough, but the real topper is the fact that the three-month rental leases most people had signed at the beginning of August are expiring November 1. So amidst the general chaos, several members of the crew have to scurry around finding new places to live for "an unspecified additional number of days . . ." a vague situation that potential landlords aren't too crazy about.

November 6

Every day the whole place is getting more randy and difficult to manage. At the end of each day, there's Columbia, counting heads and dollars. A birthday party given by Robert Shaw's daughter, Penny, and sound technician, Mick Harris, became the setting for a free-for-all between two very unlikely combatants on the British crew: mild-mannered, bookish sound recorder Robin Gregory and a sturdy, compact "spark" (lighting man) named Derek Gatrell. However the brawl originated, it ended with Derek being the recipient of a big shiner. The entire British crew has begun whistling old English ballads in unison as they set up shots on Treece's set, a melodic statement of restiveness that resounds through the stage like an outtake from *The Bridge on the River Kwai*. And they celebrated the completion of work on the Orange Grove motel room set by thoughtfully striking the set . . . something like the way Stanley Kowalski cleared the table for Stella in *A Streetcar Named Desire*. Every piece of scaffolding, every prop, even every pane of glass was demolished in an exuberant orgy of destruction.

Across the Atlantic Ocean in the United States, Jimmy Carter has been elected President in a dramatic grand finale to his astonishing campaign. On *The Deep*, this significant event goes all but unnoticed. Oh, we've heard about it, all right, but it seems extremely remote. How could even a brilliant peanut-farming politician becoming President compare to the trials and tribulations of blowing up a lighthouse, decapitating an arch-villain, and sinking a ship—twice? "Hey, didja hear, Carter was elected," someone says, and the reply is, "Yeah . . . where are we shooting tomorrow?"

Not that we're not patriotic. If patriotism is measured by a desire to be in your own country, then by now we're all arch-chauvinists. Especially since lovely little Bermuda is no longer such a bed of roses. Summertime is over, and it's cold. Frigid, moist weather has made our summer wardrobes unwearable and our mobylettes—the transportation on which many of the team depend—unbearable. "Deepers" who were freezing in T-shirts and cut-offs keep the local English woolens shops in business. Wind blows. Rain falls. Many locals muse that the weather is so unusually bad it's like "February in November." And having been in Bermuda in February during our first location trip, I know it's the awful truth. Daylight Savings Time was turned back, night falls at 4:30 P.M. and so does the temperature, and the whole enterprise is becoming a dreadful grind.

Nowhere is the wintry weather less appreciated than up at the underwater set. Even the difficult summer filming at the B.U.S. in retrospect seems like Paradise Lost compared to what we face now. No one had dreamed that the black tarpaulin which served to cool the set in August would end up serving the completely opposite function—protection from the biting winter winds which are sometimes seventy knots—that now whip across the top of the bluff.

Getting into the cold, murky water of the set in weather like this for hours every day is sheer agony. Cold has a strange effect on divers. Along with everything else, it numbs concentration and slows down the thought processes, a particularly grim circumstance when now, more than ever, we need all our wits about us to get what we need on film and get out of the BUS for good. In a season of snowmen and chestnuts roasting over open fires and the like, an underwater set on a rocky Bermuda hill is positively the last place anyone really wants to be. But our crew, actors, doubles, and director dive and dive and dive again . . .

Full wetsuits are now *de rigeur* for the whole team as they try every possible way to cope with the cold. And not only full wetsuits, but sometimes *two* complete wetsuits, one on top of the other; accessorized with vests, booties, gloves, hood. Underneath the whole ensemble, many members have discovered that ordinary women's panty hose provide an extra insulating layer that seems to help retain heat. All this, with mask, tank, and twice as many weights as usual because all that extra rubber makes a diver bob up in the water like a cork—and it's a toss-up whether the team members look more like astronauts or children bundled up by overprotective mothers.

Laden down with all this paraphernalia, the team lumbers into the set, and they're fine . . . for about the first minute. Then a tiny trickle of ice-cold water finds its way in, cutting down the back and around the body like a razor until the whole torso is encased in a layer of freezing brine. Finally, the water warms to body temperature, and then for a while, a diver is OK . . . but only for a while, until he or she starts shivering uncontrollably after being in that cruel environment for nearly an hour straight.

The Gorillas emerge from the water between setups chilled to the bone. They have to warm up fast since they have to go down again in just minutes. Air conditioners in the work shacks have now become heaters, and two huge hot water heaters and plastic coverings now warm the showers. With all that wetsuiting on, there's no time for team members to strip down for a hot shower between set-ups. But Al Giddings has discovered something just as good. Al turns the hot water in the shower on full blast, lifting one wetsuited arm up to the nozzle and tucking his sleeve near the wrist over it. The hot water runs into the wetsuit, turning it into one huge hot water bottle. Standing in those showers basking in that hot water has become everyone's favored pastime during these last weeks at the BUS. We're now even holding all our skull sessions right there.

If the sturdy, experienced underwater team has to go through all this just to be able to function in the cold waters of the set, you can believe that diving is surely no joy for our cast these days, especially delicate Jacqueline Bisset. Not only are our actors simply not as used to working in frigid waters as the Gorillas are; they're also forced to continue wearing the summery, minimal diving outfits they'd worn during filming months before. It's like working in the frozen Alaskan tundra in underwear.

A recurring nightmare of mine is that one day our stars will just rebel and refuse to climb back into that set. Even Peter Yates has ample cause by this time to just forget the whole thing and let Percy the Eel eat his Directors Guild card. To spare our cast unnecessary time underwater, everything is planned even more carefully than ever. That way, our stars can go down, do two takes in quick succession, come up and get warm, zip over to another set for some work, then come back some hours later for one more dive.

Somehow, working in this sporadic fashion, we have

finally completed the underwater work with our three principals.

For our fourth principal, Lou Gossett, the fun is just about to begin. Cloche's—and Percy's—moment of truth is at hand.

Months ago, when we began designing Percy the Eel in Los Angeles, our first priority, of course, was that he be able to bite. But as our eel research grew, it almost began to look like we'd bitten off more than we could chew. As I've mentioned, if our moray was to be really authentic, he had to be able to do several things. He had to be able to move in and out of his eel hole; from side to side; up and down; and he would have to breathe. Certain mechanical animals can be filmed from some distance away, but not ours. The whole scene will be shot in tight close-up, and since the camera will have to be just a few feet away the whole time, our eel will have to perform his duties gracefully and convincingly.

No matter how cleverly you design and build a cinematic mechanical creature, there are always unforeseeable snags in its operation. Witness the makers of the new *King Kong,* working with a mechanical gorilla arm on a large, brightly lit sound stage where even the simplest motion was still a nightmare to execute. We're doing the same type of work—underwater. One of the things that made our task easier, or so we originally thought, was the fact that Percy lives in a hole, which meant he could be directly operated from behind by stunt divers. But it also means that those divers will actually have to be *inside* the hole, operating in a dark, claustrophobic space from which they won't even be able to see what the eel is doing on the other side! Not only is the situation incredibly confining, but water itself affects movement strangely. Some things get heavier in water, others lighter. Water resistance ensures that nothing will move as agilely, or quickly, or with as much control as is possible on land. With built-in complications like these, our Percy had to be as simple to operate as possible.

Walter and Charlie began by building some of Percy's movement capacity right into his skeleton.

Since Percy moves in a relatively limited fashion—he doesn't have to tie himself in knots, for example (something which moray eels do to get anchored for an attack)—they could build a straight spine for him. Attached to this, about half a foot apart, were eight round stainless steel ribs, set up to move back and forth in a predetermined way to give Percy the undulating movement he requires. Over these ribs, plastic strips were laid along the length of Percy's body to make the movement even more fluid, and to prevent the ribs from being visible through his water-resistant dive-suit sponge flesh and neoprene rubber skin.

14
DEEPEST CHALLENGES

To make Percy move, Walter and Charlie set out to build as compact a system as possible. Percy's brain and central nervous system are a close series of air cylinders and hydraulic rams that take up, amazingly, a mere eight inches of space in his body, right behind his fiberglass skull and hinged jaws. Since Percy's workings are so economical, he needs all the help he can get from the human divers controlling his movements. Long steel rods from his hydraulic system run lengthwise through his body and out his open back end to a series of levers. These are attached to a dolly on which a special effects diver stationed in the eel hole can sit as if on a lawn mower or tractor. The dolly moves on bronze wheels on a stainless steel track, the same materials used in all of Percy's moving parts to prevent rust. Percy's up-and-down motion is controlled by pressing a pedal with the left foot. For left and right motions, the diver has a rudder, much like that used for steering a glider, which directly controls Percy's side-to-side movement. An air cylinder assist creates "power steering" to prevent the diver's arms from growing tired.

For Percy's in-and-out movements, the only power employed is good old manpower. Four more divers, two stationed on each side of the dolly, will actually push it and pull it along the track on cue, thus creating Percy's lunging motion. Between water resistance and the lack of good footing in the hole, it's no easy job. And it's so cramped that Walter and Charlie don't even have room to design handles or grips for the dolly.

The divers just have to grab onto the sides and give it the old heave-ho.

Everything these five divers do still doesn't include two very important functions for our giant eel: breathing and biting. Eels have a rather unique way of breathing. The moray opens his mouth to inhale oxygen through the water. As the excess water is exhaled, it ripples and bellows out under the skin before being passed out through the gills—in the eel's case, small round holes on the side of the head. It's a complete cycle: open mouth, ripples, close mouth, open mouth—over and over, about twenty-five times a minute. Walter Stones had never done anything *exactly* like it, but he had done something similar, at least mechanically speaking. In the forties and fifties, when the film studios needed side shots of their hero galloping along during westerns but didn't actually want to put the actor on a real horse where he might break his neck, Walter created, naturally, mechanical horses. These "galloped" in place on special platforms, complete with shoulder muscles rippling under the skin as they ran. This under-the-skin rippling was a problem similar to Percy's breathing, and Walter solved both in a similar way—with a steel frame which would regularly expand and contract, rhythmically inflating and deflating the skin. In Percy's case, this motion, linked to the opening and closing of the jaws to create the total breathing pattern, is controlled by an electrically driven motor on the surface. This motor is connected to Percy via cable and manned by two *more* special-effects staffers.

Percy's biggest job had yet to be tackled: his bite. Since both breathing and biting involve opening and closing the jaws, the two motions would be controlled by the same mechanism. But the bite had to be a much bigger movement. And Percy must be able to breathe when he's not biting. Another problem still: the men in the eel hole can't even see what's going on outside the hole, so how can they possibly know when to activate the eel bite?

The obvious reply is, they can't. So the situation calls for someone who can. This seventh person, stationed out of shooting range next to the camera, will control Percy's biting mechanism with a special hydraulic cylinder set-up. When Percy and Cloche are precisely in place, he'll pull up and push down on the cylinder. This action will instantaneously overrule the breathing mechanism, and Percy will bite right on cue. A built-in safety trap will let his jaws close only so far, to prevent real harm being done to the human head in their grasp.

Even with the assurance of a safety trap, diving into cold, murky water to put your head into a mechanical eel's mouth is not many people's idea of a good time. Lou Gosset's stunt double Richard Washington, who really has the worst of it, doesn't pretend to enjoy having to spend hours every day down there. But he's done the job well and without complaint. In fact, Washington seems most unhappy not with the work itself, but with the fact that he had to shave his head to match Gosset's bald pate!

Even with the shaved head, though, Richard isn't a perfect match for Lou. Water does strange things to skin color. And though Richard is black, for some reason he looks utterly bleached out in the dailies. We knew something had to be done when Columbia called us and demanded, "Hey, are you guys nuts, using a white double for Lou Gosset?" So make-up man Eddie Henriques came to the rescue once again, this time with "blackface" (actually heavy, waterproof deep-brown makeup) to be completely applied to Washington before he sets foot in the water. Richard is also eight inches shorter than rangy ex-basketball star Gosset, who measures in at 6'4". We couldn't exactly put lifts in his flippers, so there wasn't much to do but stick to head-on camera angles to minimize the difference between the two.

So here we all are in the middle of November, still slaving away on our big eel climax, in our big underwater set, which is now a big pain in the ass. The sun is setting not much after 4 P.M., and our team often continues to work with lights in otherwise complete darkness, sometimes till eight in the evening. By this time, weekends are a relic of the past, forsaken in the rush to get the film done. The team has worked for three straight weeks without one day's break. To put it mildly, it's not anyone's idea of Hollywood glamor.

Not only do we have to get the bite and the attendant necessary special effects, like blood, done right, but we also have a brand new special effect dreamed up by Yates in the middle of production: a sensational idea, but a nightmare to do. Yates thought a shot of Cloche's mask shattering as the eel's jaws bite down on it would be a terrific touch, and we all agreed. So Ira Anderson, our special effects man, got to work on it. Ira has done dozens of explosions in his time, but this was probably his smallest ever. He's rigged a face mask with several tiny charges which, on cue, will explode it as the jaws close.

Now we have the fight, the bite, the blood, and the exploding mask to coordinate, and none of it is coming easily. The total manpower—or eelpower—necessary to make this single shot is incredible. It includes five divers in the dark eel lair; two more on the surface; one diver behind the camera controlling the bite; two cinematographers wielding their Petermar cameras; four key lighting men; one diver handling the blood squirting from the "squish" head; another diver working the exploding mask effect; underwater prop man Peter Grant using his own hand to simulate Cloche's death grip around Shaw, whose own hands are locked around the dummy head's neck; Peter Lake shooting 16mm footage of it all for a documentary about the making of *The Deep;* script girl Geri Murphy handling continuity, and me watching . . . all in a ten by twelve-foot chamber in 62-degree water!

A director's nightmare! Peter Yates, trying to choreograph the sequence (which, of course, has to be perfectly timed), had to deal with the delays of our underwater communication system, which routed his voice topside before it could be broadcast down to the crew. The blood lines broke, leaking blood too soon or too late and in the wrong places. The blood itself coagulated and clouded and turned black in the water. The pressure of the eel's jaws, fine for humans, was too light for the dummy head and had to be readjusted. The mask blew up before the jaws closed. Then we ran out of diving safety plastic and had to redo the gag with glass, which explodes at a different rate, which meant new timing. It was one thing after another, an ultimately uncontrollable situation that all the skull sessions in the world couldn't prepare us for. We ended up shooting thousands upon thousands of feet of film before finally doing Cloche in to Yates' satisfaction. And since the end of Cloche meant, at last, the end of filming on this scene, not one of us was sorry to see him go.

During its last few weeks of filming, *The Deep* is in the disaster business. Our shooting schedule seems made up of one cinematic cataclysm after another. We have to crash the Orange Grove elevator. We have to destroy the *Goliath* twice: crash her at the beginning of the film, and explode her off the reef where she lies at the end. And we have to explode Treece's lighthouse —probably our single most spectacular stunt.

There's a funny mystique to movie explosions. In a way, they represent the whole filmmaking process. An explosion is an unpredictable, one-time-only event. It's weeks of work and worry; then *boom!* It's done . . . and over. A moment of pure exhilaration, followed by acute concern: do we have it on film? And then, an odd sense of letdown, and the unspoken question: could we have done it better?

Ira Anderson, Jr., the talented special effects man who'd already designed our many complicated visual "gags," has been joined during these last weeks of filming by none other than his father, Ira Anderson, Sr., himself a veteran special effects man with thirty-seven years in the business. The Andersons make a terrific team. Dad worked on all the old Abbott and Costello films, Amos and Andy, and scores of other films and television work. Ira Jr. worked on films like

Cat Ballou, Silent Movie, and five of Peter Yates' previous films. Together, father and son's experience combined adds up to half a century of special effects work, and in that time the Andersons have done every kind of film stunt you can imagine. Both enjoy a well-done crash or explosion more than just about anything, and during the last few weeks of our filming, they'll have plenty to keep them happily busy. The first order of business is to blow up Treece's lighthouse.

In the script, Treece, furious over Kevin's death (you recall, we left him hanging, all broken up as Treece discovers him), sets out with David and Gail to blow up the *Goliath* once and for all. Coffin watches them go, then races up to the lighthouse tower, where he knows the ampules are stored. What he doesn't know is that the light was booby-trapped earlier by Treece, David, and Kevin, to prevent anyone from getting the drugs. Coffin rips open the door and trips the switch, blowing himself and the tower to smithereens. Treece, David, and Gail are cascaded with debris as they are about to leave from Treece's dock.

November 8

So the Andersons began gathering the necessary explosives. Meanwhile, construction supervisor Dick Frift's team went to work weakening the top structure and simultaneously strengthening the tower floor so that the explosion will travel up, not down. And back at Dockyard, George Justin, Peter Yates and I tried to figure out just when to schedule this extravaganza. In the story, the explosion takes place in the early hours of morning, so some overcast will be all right to represent the pre-dawn glow in the sky. But if it's too overcast, there won't be enough light for the high-speed cameras we'll be using to get our slow motion shots. And we can't have too much wind, which would make the explosion not just difficult to control visually, but that much more dangerous to boot. The weather is none too great these days and shows no signs of improving, but we have to get the explosion done. So reluctantly, during this depressingly cloudy week, we've scheduled our Coney Island explosion for Thursday, November 8.

Sure enough, the eighth dawned cloudy. But there was light in the sky and it didn't look like rain, so the company grouped at Coney Island. The Andersons began laying their "powder." By now father and son had come up with a special "recipe" for our explosion (each one calls for something different). This one required 500 feet of explosive-filled cord, fourteen pounds of explosive powder and hand-made bombs, twenty-six sticks of dynamite, eleven gallons of rubber cement, and fifteen gallons of gasoline.

When you're blowing something up, once has to be enough; so you have to make sure you have as much coverage as is humanly possible. Chris Challis supervised the positioning of five cameras at strategic points all over the island to capture the explosion on film. Production stills of the explosion were necessary too, and Keith Hamshere and Peter Lake had motor-driven Nikons on tripods and in the hands of willing company volunteers all over Coney Island to capture the moment on Tri-X film. Photographers lined up behind the far jetty facing the lighthouse, looking like guerrillas in trenches.

Anticipation alternated with boredom as 1 P.M.— the scheduled explosion time—came and went. The sky began to darken ominously and it became a race between the Andersons and the weather. Would they finish their work before the light of day was lost?

Then a new crisis reared its head. We'd tried to keep word of the explosion as quiet as possible, since it would be logistically nightmarish and dangerous for Coney Island to be swarming with people as we tried to blow it up. But word of the explosion had somehow leaked out and it was being *broadcast* on Bermuda radio! Police kept the curious sightseers off Coney Island, but hundreds and hundreds of them quickly lined the banks across the bay. Local television cameras and newspapers were now on hand for the big moment.

The Andersons finished their work at three o'clock

in the afternoon. But now the sky was completely covered with clouds, and too dark to make the shot. It didn't exactly look like the kind of sky that would brighten up—especially in Bermuda, where once the afternoon clouds of autumn roll in, they never roll out again. But Bermuda law forbade our leaving the explosives overnight, and to have to dismantle them and reschedule the blow-up would be disaster. We needed permission from just about every department agency and regulatory body in Bermuda's bureaucracy to do this shot.

Yates and I decided that no matter what, we were going to blow up that lighthouse *today!* Time was just too precious, and far too short. We all but implored the sky—maybe, if it was just going to get worse, we should go ahead and do it now, whether it was too dark or not. But way off in the distance, we saw a bright patch, where the clouds were much thinner and the light showed through. A little luck . . . Boy did we need it now! Justin kept his fingers and toes crossed.

All eyes were riveted onto this patch of sky as it began to move. It was coming our way! Hallelujah! Chris Challis grabbed the bullhorn and ordered the camera operators to stand by. Minutes passed. And then the thin patch floated right over the lighthouse, making the sky the perfect backdrop for the explosion. It was a miracle! I half expected to hear a heavenly choir from above. Chris yelled to the camera operators and, one by one, they replied, "Speed . . ." They were rolling, all over the island. The motor-driven still cameras were posed for action. Everything was ready, and Derek Cracknell, boomed *"Action!"*

There was an initial bang, and then a deafening explosion rang out that shot the top cap of the lighthouse 150 feet into the air while fiery pieces of debris rained down onto the island. The top of the lighthouse landed back on the decapitated lighthouse column, then came rolling down the hill in a fireball, which smoldered until being extinguished by the firemen who'd been standing by.

No sooner had the explosion been completed than the sky darkened and rain poured down. We'd made it just in time! Everyone congratulated the Andersons on a spectacular job. "Yeah, it went off pretty nice," Ira Anderson, Sr. modestly replied. But we were jubilant.

Now, both in the story and in the production, it was the *Goliath* wreck's turn to meet its own spectacular end. Blown up by Treece, it tumbles off its underwater cliff into eternal oblivion hundreds of feet below. Ira Anderson, with full wetsuit on, rigged special little charges inside the ship's hull. Eight levers which would trigger the charges were linked to the model's surface with a series of special wires. Since a large, 310-foot wreck would take much longer to explode and crash over a thousand-foot ledge than an eight-foot model over a 20-foot one, the action had to be slowed down considerably by filming at very high speed—seventy-four frames per second instead of the usual twenty-four.

At the moment of truth, our B.U.S. was the scene of yet another spectacular explosion . . . so spectacular that those of us watching had to remind ourselves that it was actually happening on a small scale. The ship bucked and rocked, splitting apart at the special seams which had been worked into its design to fall apart quickly upon impact. Red explosions flickered in the windows of the ship as it tumbled off the edge of the abyss, into the deep . . . a memorable finale for the ship which provided the setting for the most important action of our story. Treece's tiny figure emerging from the wreck just in time will be created later via our matte optical process.

But that wasn't the end of the *Goliath;* not yet . . . at least, not for the production.

The original World War II crash of the *Goliath* onto Bermuda's reefs opens the novel *The Deep* and was retained in the script as a vivid beginning for the film. The scene had also been rewritten to visually establish some important plot information. The sequence now introduces young Adam Coffin and the ampules of morphine, efficiently and dramatically, by showing the young Coffin struggling frantically to lash down the boxes of ampules as the fateful storm rages outside, moments before the ship goes down.

November 12

There was no way we could afford to actually crash an entire ship, so the crash of the *Goliath* would have to be handled impressionistically, with cleverly designed sets and a large helping of Hollywood magic. Two key sets were conceived and designed: the lower hold in which Coffin is trying to store the morphine, and the ship's bridge, in which the captain and the first mate are stationed, fighting the storm. Too late, they realize they are headed right toward a treacherous reef. The ship smashes up onto the reefs as the captain makes a last-ditch attempt to steer the craft. His arm, caught in the wildly spinning spokes of the wheel, is torn off with sickening suddenness at the elbow, and the captain is pitched by a high wave into the sea.

To film this, whoever played the captain would actually have to be tossed off the set—and that was certainly dangerous enough to require the services of an experienced stunt man. So though veteran actor Cameron Mitchell is our captain, stunt man Howard Curtis will double him in that final shot.

Ira Anderson and Eddie Henriques have been huddling on the spinning wheel and prosthetic arm we would need to do the sequence. Peter Benchley has returned to Bermuda to do a cameo as the first mate. For the scene of Adam Coffin in the lower hold, Eli Wallach's son will again enact the young Coffin, with Al Giddings and Howard Curtis playing themselves in the chamber with him as ship's mates. We'll cut to this scene after the captain is pitched overboard to fully establish the fate of the ship.

November 14

A huge old aviation hangar has become our third sound stage by this time, and now holds our lower hold set. Today it was a mighty strange scene, as we finally filmed this sequence. The lower hold set took the form of a large, open-topped box perched on a gigantic rocker, on which it could roll from side to side. It rested at a 45–degree angle from the ground as crew members crawled over it like ants. Yates and I hovered at the top of the set watching the action from above. Three cameras were set up at strategic points around the set, including one of Al's underwater Petermars hidden in the set itself to film the enormous tidal wave of water pouring into the hold as the ship goes down. To achieve that effect, we had to rig up a special pumping system and water chute rising thirty-five feet off the ground which, at the proper moment, would throw 15,000 gallons of water from two huge drums down a chute and into the set.

Anderson Sr. was perched at the top of the water chute when the cue was given. We had known the blast of water would be powerful, but we didn't know just *how* powerful. The water spewed into the set with a deafening roar—and with such ferocity that it knocked Ira Sr. down and almost entirely off his perch to the floor, thirty-five feet below. In the hold set, the water threw Howard Curtis to the floor and pushed Al Giddings' hand back with such force that he ripped it on the metal lining of the set.

The bridge scene was even more dramatic in its execution. The bridge was a 6,000-pound set built twenty-five feet off the ground on a huge wooden hemisphere to create the rocking and rolling effect of a ship in storm. Again we had to create a ferocious wall of water—this one to knock Howard Curtis right out of the set. Four fire hoses, two wind machines, and again a special 35-foot water chute which would discharge 12,000 gallons of water through the set, were set up.

For this scene, we couldn't rely on the protective environment of a sound stage. It had to be shot as an exterior, and it had to be shot at night. When we began filming last evening, it was very cold and damp, and though we needed rain and wind, we had to battle to control it. Our battle against the elements was lost: it began to pour. Even though we were creating a storm for our cameras, there was no way we could film in a real one. The most crucial moment of the scene—the shot of the captain being pitched into the sea—could simply not be done. At 5:30 A.M., the production had to shut down. The drizzle continued on into the late morning, eased up, then continued. There was no way of telling when the rain would stop. Knowing Bermuda, it could be days.

But toward this evening, the rain did let up, and before it could change its mind again, the final key shot of our *Goliath* crash was set up. Again the great hemisphere on which the set rested began to move, rocking the bridge back and forth; again Howard Curtis, dressed in the captain's uniform with a bleeding stump of an arm, frantically began to try to get control of the ship. Again water began to pummel the set furiously. And this time, right on schedule, the captain lost his balance and was pitched with a spine-chilling scream out the door into the sea . . . in reality, into the mattresses and cardboard boxes secured around the set twenty feet below to break Curtis' fall.

Essentially, the crash of the *Goliath* marked the end of filming. We spent a few more days on inserts and pickups; then, lacking the time, money, or energy for the wrap party which traditionally celebrates the end of filming, we've wearily packed up and gone home. But in the story, with *our* final scene—the crash of the *Goliath*—the whole adventure called *The Deep* was just beginning.

15

THE DEEP SURFACES

9,885 dives, 10,780 man hours underwater, 1,054,000 cubic feet of compressed air, four oceans, and 151 days after it began, the main production phase of *The Deep* has been completed. But the film is far from finished. All we now have is raw material—a lot of it. Underwater material had been almost always shot with three cameras at once; first and second units had been filming simultaneously for months. Those thousands and thousands of feet of footage now have to be shaped into a finished film.

The editing team had been working on the production all during filming, and have now regrouped in Connecticut, where Peter Yates lives. They've edited there for ten weeks before coming back to Hollywood to complete the work. The bone-numbing New England winter was quite a change both from Bermuda and from Los Angeles, where our editors live. In addition to Peter Yates and editor Bob Wolfe, we have a new film editor, David Berlatsky, a director. Both soft-spoken, unassuming, and excellent at their work, Bob and David are a great editorial team. Assistant editors Mike Klein and Carol Jackson are also on hand to organize and keep tabs on the mountain of footage we've generated. Robert Shaw's daughter Penny, interested in film production as a career, has joined the team as an apprentice assistant editor. What she lacks in experience, she makes up in a quick mind and an eagerness to work. With this editing team, *The Deep* is in good hands.

Editing is a crucial phase in the making of a motion picture—maybe even *the* crucial phase. Here is where the movie actually takes shape. A scene can have several totally different meanings or feelings, just depending on how it's edited. By extension, so can an entire film. Lines of dialogue can be added or dropped. The pace can be quickened, or significant pauses can be added. Plot points can be emphasized or made more subtle . . . all to the good or detriment of the total film. The script, of course, has set certain guidelines, but in the editing these become tremendously flexible. And the alternatives can be dizzying, especially since every change, every cut, affects something somewhere else.

In the film, for example, when David and Gail first bring Treece the ampule they discovered in the *Goliath,* he takes it from them without their knowledge. Now, that can be shown in a close-up. Then the audience will see what Treece is doing. But then he might look like a thief. Or he might have taken it for their own protection. His action might seem clumsily obvious in close-up. Or David and Gail might seem ridiculously unobservant for not having noticed. On the other hand, if Yates uses the long shot, most of the audience may not see it, and they won't learn until later, along with David and Gail, that Treece had taken the ampule. That could work, but the net effect could either be suspense and revelation, or just confusion and irritation. Besides all these specific variables, there's the intangible total quality a scene must have: how does the scene *feel?*

Those are just a few of the choices which a tiny moment in a relatively straightforward simple interior set scene presents. Imagine hundreds of those choices, many far more complex and *all* affecting each other, and you get an idea of the magnitude of the job.

There are other problems. As the preliminary rough cut was assembled, Yates and the team realized that, in spite of the many inserts we'd filmed, we needed still more. Inserts are extreme close-ups which help detail the action and provide variety and texture in the editing. When our three heroes are "treasure sleuthing"— researching the history of the *Grifon's* treasure—we wanted inserts of hands turning book pages, close-ups of shipping manifests, the charred silver coin being studied under a magnifying glass, and so on. Some of these and others had been done, but some had not, and now is the time to do them.

With the huge variety of water conditions in all the different bodies of water we'd worked in, much of the underwater footage varies wildly in color and brightness. That's not only a difficult distraction during editing; it also means a lot of time and money to be spent on laboratory work to correct these flaws and to balance the whole print. All our footage has to have the same colorful yet mysterious quality. Also vital to the success of our underwater scenes are those panoramic views of swimmers going by the *Goliath,* lying on the edge of its underwater cliff, which we'd hoped to accomplish with optical mattes.

But it just hasn't worked out that way. Several technical difficulties are involved in this exacting technique, and even after months of trying we've never managed to solve them all. Finally Tony Masters suggested going to animation. Carefully painted tiny figures will be brought to life on hundreds of cells (clear plastic animation sheets). These will then be laid over our model footage and the two will be photographed together, frame by frame, to give the effect we need. So a vital series of underwater shots has become a postproduction problem, and while our editors know roughly how the final footage would look, they still have to wing it, more or less, until the process has been completed.

All our underwater footage had been shot MOS—without sound—presenting yet another challenge since the final underwater sequences will have an as-yet unprepared sound track. ("At least the editing room is a lot more peaceful than it was during the editing of *Bullitt,*" Peter Yates observed.) As the underwater scenes took shape it was obvious that the more underwater dialogue we could work in, the better. So new dialogue will have to be written, recorded, and then "looped"—carefully timed and laid into the sound track. And since our underwater dialogue will still be relatively brief, we want to exploit the sound effects possibilities of *The Deep* to the fullest. The hollow sound of breathing amplified by scuba gear. The whoosh of the water current, like being inside a huge seashell. The delicate tinkling sound of the slender glass ampules as they're gathered. The eerie groaning of the shipwreck as it shifts position in its sea bed.

During production, our sound recorder Robin Gregory, (*2,001*) was asked to try to capture a library of authentic ocean sea effects for us. Robin, of course, turned to Teddy Tucker, who promptly whisked him out on a diving trip to the *Constellation,* the real-life, drug-laden *Goliath* inspiration. When it went down, the *Constellation* split in two and its innards—boilers, pumps, and the like—came spewing out of the hull, where they're continually moved back and forth by the current. "She's always groaning and whining and sighing; it's the spookiest sound you ever heard," Teddy had told us. So Robin, who, happily, knew how to dive, took a water-proofed tape recorder into the Atlantic and captured the spine-tingling sounds of the *Constellation* for us.

With the general, ongoing sound of the ocean (or, in technical industry lingo, the ocean "presence"), Robin had more trouble. Since sound equipment functions differently than the human ear, what sounds to the ear like a haunting, hollow sound comes off on tape exactly like, in Robin's words, "the hiss of frying bacon." So Robin had to exercise some ingenuity above and beyond the call of duty. He took the sound of the ocean, both from above the surface and below, and added the whispering sound of wind in the Bermuda trees. He then proceeded to work with these sounds, slowing them down, dubbing them over each other, rerecording them several times, electronically diffusing the sound, to achieve just the right effect. With the end of filming, Robin's job was technically over; so, for our postproduction phase, an excellent sound effects mixer and cutter named Fred Brown, who had done an incredible job with the potent and frightening sound

effects of *The Exorcist,* is taking over to meld and
build our sound track.

The single most important "sound effect" in a film is
that created by its musical score. A terrific score can
enhance a film immeasurably; the music and the visuals combine to create something entirely new. Music
is especially important in *The Deep* to lend mood and
texture to our long underwater scenes. So now, on the
eve of postproduction, we suddenly have to solve what
is properly a preproduction consideration.

Coincidence may once again save *The Deep.*

My company, FilmWorks, has just merged with
Casablanca Records, a well-known independent record company, to create Casablanca Record and Film-
Works, Inc.. As if I didn't have enough on my mind
during our last weeks of production, I've also been busy
hammering out a multi-media corporate merger! And
since the ink has just dried on our agreement I've recruited my new partner Neil Bogart and his people in
the search for a new composer. Together, with our
combined industry contacts, we've launched an intensive search. We flew one prospect out to Bermuda to
actually dive in our underwater set to get a feel for the
underwater atmosphere *and* the experience of diving,
something we feel will be invaluable to anyone who
ends up as our composer. But for various reasons, that
didn't pan out. We've kept looking. No one seems
right. Yates, Neil, and I are frantic, but we're determined not to settle for anything less than the best. It's
just too important.

We didn't have to settle. The search has been happily resolved with the signing of John Barry. John
is a seasoned professional who did the musical score
for, among other notable films, *Midnight Cowboy,*
King Kong, and several of the James Bond pictures.
His powerful, haunting musical sound, wide experience, and terrific (literally) track record make him the
perfect candidate for *The Deep.* Getting such a composer on what is, after all, pretty short notice is yet
another in the whole series of happy accidents that

have helped realize this film—and which have helped convince me that, against all the odds, *The Deep* was a movie that was meant to be made.

So the fate of *The Deep* is in the hands of a whole new team of professionals. After fighting the rigors of deep sea diving, barracudas, eels, sharks, bends, wind, waves, rain, and sheer exhaustion, all our adventures . . . the product itself still ultimately boils down to a series of detailed, sometimes tedious jobs in a series of small, dark rooms. Editing. Looping dialogue. Recording and mixing the music. Recording the effects. Mixing the sound track. Correcting the color. Doing optical work. Over and over and over until everything is just right. It's all necessary to any motion picture; but after all we've been through, I thought it would be rather anticlimactic.

It isn't. And my additional anxiety over ads, trailers, radio spots, tours, bookings, and terms only masks the real trauma: Does Yates truly have a vision of how the whole film will fit together? He's been working his tail off, yet now we can only stand by impatiently to see if we have something to show for it. It's all in his hands now, and it's pure hell waiting for him to deliver it up.

As for the production team, after leaving Bermuda with the usual promises to get together and keep in touch, they have gone on to celebrate the holidays and prepare for the new year in their own individual ways. Robert Shaw went to New York, in anticipation of becoming a proud papa. Robert was the pro. He gave his aid and talent willingly and collaboratively. Jacqueline Bisset went to London for the holidays, and in June will go on to her next picture, playing a part inspired by Jackie Onassis Kennedy in *The Greek Tycoon*. She had been enormously supportive, completely open to cast and crew alike, and was loved by one and all. Nick Nolte, still besieged by film offers, returned to his ranch outside Los Angeles and agreed to star in Karel Reisz's *Dogs of War* in February. Nick had given his very best. Always on time, he was quite real and a good friend.

Lou Gossett planned a publicity tour on behalf of the noted television anthology, *Roots*. Eli Wallach went back to his New York play and prepared to star in a John Huston film, *Winter Kills*.

Stan Waterman began another of his noted and extremely popular lecture tours, and in January will go with his son Gordie, who'd worked alongside him on *The Deep*, to the far Pacific on a major dive expedition. Al Giddings went back to work on his film boat, the *Research Vessel Eagle*, and geared up along with Chuck Nicklin and some other ex-Gorillas to go to Hawaii and do a movie special on the humpback whale. Denny Breese, who'd put the final touches on a brand new wreck-detecting device during our last weeks of filming, stuck around in Bermuda for a few weeks to go treasure diving with Teddy Tucker before returning to his home and shipwreck-salvage work in North Carolina. The many other craftsmen and crew members of *The Deep* returned home to rest up from the long haul before going on to their next projects. Even Stan Jaffe decided to make a move and leave his Columbia position and form his own very successful production company.

And that's the way it is in the film industry. A film company is like a big family during production . . . one which, in spite of the close ties created over the long months together, must inevitably break up. The people who made *The Deep* will never again be all assembled together, and that's a little sad. Oh, we'll bump into each other on other films—a few at a time. Some will perhaps keep in touch; others probably won't. But one thing's for certain: we'll all see the film!

It's scheduled to open in 700 theaters all across the country on June 17, 1977. As of this date, I haven't even seen Peter Yates' rough cut of the film yet. *I* still don't know what *The Deep* will be like, much less how the public will receive it. Except for those who read this book, audiences won't know about all the time, money, energy, and love expended on this film. All they'll know is whether they like it or not. And maybe that is as it should be.

ABOUT THE AUTHOR

PETER GUBER'S decision to become an independent motion picture producer culminated an impressive eight years as an executive with Columbia Pictures. He served as Executive Vice President in charge of world-wide production during the last three years, a period in which the Columbia Pictures' feature film product reversed a downward trend and surged to record-breaking profits.

Guber's rapid ascent in the motion picture industry began in 1968 when he was recruited as an executive assistant for Columbia while pursuing his M.B.A. degree at the New York University Graduate School of Business Administration. Guber also holds a B.A. from Syracuse University, a Juris Doctor degree from the N.Y.U. School of Law, and an L.L.M. degree from the same university. He is a member of the New York, California, and D.C. bars.

As an independent filmmaker, he operated under the banner of Peter Guber's Filmworks for a period of one year, during which time he began production on *The Deep*.

In November 1976 Guber formed a partnership with the highly successful recording company, Casablanca Records, resulting in Casablanca Record and FilmWorks, Inc., of which Guber is Chairman of the Board.

The second feature film produced for the new company will be *Six Weeks*, starring Audrey Hepburn, Tatum O'Neal and Nick Nolte. Filming will begin mid-September of 1977.

Other feature film and television projects are already in preparation and will follow. In the sphere of feature film production, Peter Guber will continue to maintain a close and successful working relationship with Columbia within the framework of their long-term multiple picture deal with the studio.

In addition, drawing on his extensive motion picture production experience, Peter Guber has been a member of the faculty of UCLA where he teaches and is presently writing two books, one of which is a text dealing with the contemporary realities of the moviemaking business.

DON'T MISS
THESE CURRENT
Bantam Bestsellers

☐	DR. ATKINS DIET REVOLUTION	(11001—$2.25)
☐	HOW TO SPEAK SOUTHERN Mitchell & Rawls	(10970—$1.25)
☐	BLACK SUNDAY Thomas Harris	(10940—$2.25)
☐	DOLORES Jacqueline Susann	(10500—$1.95)
☐	THE LAST CHANCE DIET Dr. Robert Linn	(10490—$1.95)
☐	THE DEEP Peter Benchley	(10422—$2.25)
☐	VOTE FOR LOVE Barbara Cartland	(10341—$1.50)
☐	MAVREEN Claire Lorrimer	(10208—$1.95)
☐	LETTERS HOME Sylvia Plath	(10202—$2.50)
☐	THE GUINNESS BOOK OF WORLD RECORDS 15th Ed. McWhirters	(10166—$2.25)
☐	DUBAI Robin Moore	(10099—$1.95)
☐	LIFE AFTER LIFE Raymond Moody, Jr.	(10080—$1.95)
☐	DORIS DAY: HER OWN STORY A. E. Hotchner	(2888—$1.95)
☐	LINDA GOODMAN'S SUN SIGNS	(2777—$1.95)
☐	RAGTIME E. L. Doctorow	(2600—$2.25)
☐	THE EAGLE HAS LANDED Jack Higgins	(2500—$1.95)
☐	ASPEN Burt Hirschfeld	(2491—$1.95)
☐	THE MAGIC OF FINDHORN Paul Hawken	(2463—$2.25)
☐	THE MONEYCHANGERS Arthur Hailey	(2300—$1.95)
☐	HELTER SKELTER Vincent Bugliosi	(2222—$1.95)

Buy them at your local bookstore or use this handy coupon for ordering:

Bantam Books, Inc., Dept. FB, 414 East Golf Road, Des Plaines, Ill. 60016

Please send me the books I have checked above. I am enclosing $_____
(please add 50¢ to cover postage and handling). Send check or money order
—no cash or C.O.D's please.

Mr/Mrs/Miss_____

Address_____

City_____ State/Zip_____

Please allow four weeks for delivery. This offer expires 7/78.　　FB—7/77

Bantam Book Catalog

Here's your up-to-the-minute listing of every book currently available from Bantam.

This easy-to-use catalog is divided into categories and contains over 1400 titles by your favorite authors.

So don't delay—take advantage of this special opportunity to increase your reading pleasure.

Just send us your name and address and 25¢ (to help defray postage and handling costs).